THIS IS YOUR **PASSBOOK**® FOR ...

INCOME MAINTENANCE SPECIALIST

NATIONAL LEARNING CORPORATION®
passbooks.com

PASSBOOK® SERIES

THE *PASSBOOK® SERIES* has been created to prepare applicants and candidates for the ultimate academic battlefield – the examination room.

At some time in our lives, each and every one of us may be required to take an examination – for validation, matriculation, admission, qualification, registration, certification, or licensure.

Based on the assumption that every applicant or candidate has met the basic formal educational standards, has taken the required number of courses, and read the necessary texts, the *PASSBOOK® SERIES* furnishes the one special preparation which may assure passing with confidence, instead of failing with insecurity. Examination questions – together with answers – are furnished as the basic vehicle for study so that the mysteries of the examination and its compounding difficulties may be eliminated or diminished by a sure method.

This book is meant to help you pass your examination provided that you qualify and are serious in your objective.

The entire field is reviewed through the huge store of content information which is succinctly presented through a provocative and challenging approach – the question-and-answer method.

A climate of success is established by furnishing the correct answers at the end of each test.

You soon learn to recognize types of questions, forms of questions, and patterns of questioning. You may even begin to anticipate expected outcomes.

You perceive that many questions are repeated or adapted so that you can gain acute insights, which may enable you to score many sure points.

You learn how to confront new questions, or types of questions, and to attack them confidently and work out the correct answers.

You note objectives and emphases, and recognize pitfalls and dangers, so that you may make positive educational adjustments.

Moreover, you are kept fully informed in relation to new concepts, methods, practices, and directions in the field.

You discover that you arre actually taking the examination all the time: you are preparing for the examination by "taking" an examination, not by reading extraneous and/or supererogatory textbooks.

In short, this PASSBOOK®, used directedly, should be an important factor in helping you to pass your test.

INCOME MAINTENANCE SPECIALIST

DUTIES

You would provide supporting services for higher level specialists in the development and administration of income maintenance programs. These services include conducting studies, surveys and reviews; analyzing data; and preparing drafts and abstracts. You would also draft proposals for new regulations, directives and policy guidelines, write letters explaining various aspects of laws, regulation and procedures; and correspond with local social services districts on cost-effective ways to meet legal requirements. You would assist senior staff in field work and participate in the development and presentation of training programs in local districts and might supervise subordinate staff.

You would also be expected to gain or to have a thorough understanding of the automated Welfare Management System as it relates to income maintenance. This involves developing the ability to work with systems staff in enhancing existing programs or developing new ones, defining program requirements which allow the system to manipulate or generate required data; and understanding and analyzing that data.

SCOPE OF THE EXAMINATION

The written test will be designed to test for knowledge, skills, and/or abilities in such areas as:

1. Understanding and interpreting written material based on social services related documents;
2. Current issues and problems in administering social services programs;
3. Laws, rules and regulations related to income maintenance;
4. Evaluating information; and
5. Preparing written material.

HOW TO TAKE A TEST

I. YOU MUST PASS AN EXAMINATION

A. WHAT EVERY CANDIDATE SHOULD KNOW

Examination applicants often ask us for help in preparing for the written test. What can I study in advance? What kinds of questions will be asked? How will the test be given? How will the papers be graded?

As an applicant for a civil service examination, you may be wondering about some of these things. Our purpose here is to suggest effective methods of advance study and to describe civil service examinations.

Your chances for success on this examination can be increased if you know how to prepare. Those "pre-examination jitters" can be reduced if you know what to expect. You can even experience an adventure in good citizenship if you know why civil service exams are given.

B. WHY ARE CIVIL SERVICE EXAMINATIONS GIVEN?

Civil service examinations are important to you in two ways. As a citizen, you want public jobs filled by employees who know how to do their work. As a job seeker, you want a fair chance to compete for that job on an equal footing with other candidates. The best-known means of accomplishing this two-fold goal is the competitive examination.

Exams are widely publicized throughout the nation. They may be administered for jobs in federal, state, city, municipal, town or village governments or agencies.

Any citizen may apply, with some limitations, such as the age or residence of applicants. Your experience and education may be reviewed to see whether you meet the requirements for the particular examination. When these requirements exist, they are reasonable and applied consistently to all applicants. Thus, a competitive examination may cause you some uneasiness now, but it is your privilege and safeguard.

C. HOW ARE CIVIL SERVICE EXAMS DEVELOPED?

Examinations are carefully written by trained technicians who are specialists in the field known as "psychological measurement," in consultation with recognized authorities in the field of work that the test will cover. These experts recommend the subject matter areas or skills to be tested; only those knowledges or skills important to your success on the job are included. The most reliable books and source materials available are used as references. Together, the experts and technicians judge the difficulty level of the questions.

Test technicians know how to phrase questions so that the problem is clearly stated. Their ethics do not permit "trick" or "catch" questions. Questions may have been tried out on sample groups, or subjected to statistical analysis, to determine their usefulness.

Written tests are often used in combination with performance tests, ratings of training and experience, and oral interviews. All of these measures combine to form the best-known means of finding the right person for the right job.

II. HOW TO PASS THE WRITTEN TEST

A. NATURE OF THE EXAMINATION

To prepare intelligently for civil service examinations, you should know how they differ from school examinations you have taken. In school you were assigned certain definite pages to read or subjects to cover. The examination questions were quite detailed and usually emphasized memory. Civil service exams, on the other hand, try to discover your present ability to perform the duties of a position, plus your potentiality to learn these duties. In other words, a civil service exam attempts to predict how successful you will be. Questions cover such a broad area that they cannot be as minute and detailed as school exam questions.

In the public service similar kinds of work, or positions, are grouped together in one "class." This process is known as *position-classification*. All the positions in a class are paid according to the salary range for that class. One class title covers all of these positions, and they are all tested by the same examination.

B. FOUR BASIC STEPS

1) Study the announcement

How, then, can you know what subjects to study? Our best answer is: "Learn as much as possible about the class of positions for which you've applied." The exam will test the knowledge, skills and abilities needed to do the work.

Your most valuable source of information about the position you want is the official exam announcement. This announcement lists the training and experience qualifications. Check these standards and apply only if you come reasonably close to meeting them.

The brief description of the position in the examination announcement offers some clues to the subjects which will be tested. Think about the job itself. Review the duties in your mind. Can you perform them, or are there some in which you are rusty? Fill in the blank spots in your preparation.

Many jurisdictions preview the written test in the exam announcement by including a section called "Knowledge and Abilities Required," "Scope of the Examination," or some similar heading. Here you will find out specifically what fields will be tested.

2) Review your own background

Once you learn in general what the position is all about, and what you need to know to do the work, ask yourself which subjects you already know fairly well and which need improvement. You may wonder whether to concentrate on improving your strong areas or on building some background in your fields of weakness. When the announcement has specified "some knowledge" or "considerable knowledge," or has used adjectives like "beginning principles of..." or "advanced ... methods," you can get a clue as to the number and difficulty of questions to be asked in any given field. More questions, and hence broader coverage, would be included for those subjects which are more important in the work. Now weigh your strengths and weaknesses against the job requirements and prepare accordingly.

3) Determine the level of the position

Another way to tell how intensively you should prepare is to understand the level of the job for which you are applying. Is it the entering level? In other words, is this the position in which beginners in a field of work are hired? Or is it an intermediate or advanced level? Sometimes this is indicated by such words as "Junior" or "Senior" in the class title. Other jurisdictions use Roman numerals to designate the level – Clerk I, Clerk II, for example. The word "Supervisor" sometimes appears in the title. If the level is not indicated by the title, check the description of duties. Will you be working under very close supervision, or will you have responsibility for independent decisions in this work?

4) Choose appropriate study materials

Now that you know the subjects to be examined and the relative amount of each subject to be covered, you can choose suitable study materials. For beginning level jobs, or even advanced ones, if you have a pronounced weakness in some aspect of your training, read a modern, standard textbook in that field. Be sure it is up to date and has general coverage. Such books are normally available at your library, and the librarian will be glad to help you locate one. For entry-level positions, questions of appropriate difficulty are chosen – neither highly advanced questions, nor those too simple. Such questions require careful thought but not advanced training.

If the position for which you are applying is technical or advanced, you will read more advanced, specialized material. If you are already familiar with the basic principles of your field, elementary textbooks would waste your time. Concentrate on advanced textbooks and technical periodicals. Think through the concepts and review difficult problems in your field.

These are all general sources. You can get more ideas on your own initiative, following these leads. For example, training manuals and publications of the government agency which employs workers in your field can be useful, particularly for technical and professional positions. A letter or visit to the government department involved may result in more specific study suggestions, and certainly will provide you with a more definite idea of the exact nature of the position you are seeking.

III. KINDS OF TESTS

Tests are used for purposes other than measuring knowledge and ability to perform specified duties. For some positions, it is equally important to test ability to make adjustments to new situations or to profit from training. In others, basic mental abilities not dependent on information are essential. Questions which test these things may not appear as pertinent to the duties of the position as those which test for knowledge and information. Yet they are often highly important parts of a fair examination. For very general questions, it is almost impossible to help you direct your study efforts. What we can do is to point out some of the more common of these general abilities needed in public service positions and describe some typical questions.

1) General information

Broad, general information has been found useful for predicting job success in some kinds of work. This is tested in a variety of ways, from vocabulary lists to questions about current events. Basic background in some field of work, such as sociology or economics, may be sampled in a group of questions. Often these are principles which have become familiar to most persons through exposure rather than through formal training. It is difficult to advise you how to study for these questions; being alert to the world around you is our best suggestion.

2) Verbal ability

An example of an ability needed in many positions is verbal or language ability. Verbal ability is, in brief, the ability to use and understand words. Vocabulary and grammar tests are typical measures of this ability. Reading comprehension or paragraph interpretation questions are common in many kinds of civil service tests. You are given a paragraph of written material and asked to find its central meaning.

3) Numerical ability

Number skills can be tested by the familiar arithmetic problem, by checking paired lists of numbers to see which are alike and which are different, or by interpreting charts and graphs. In the latter test, a graph may be printed in the test booklet which you are asked to use as the basis for answering questions.

4) Observation

A popular test for law-enforcement positions is the observation test. A picture is shown to you for several minutes, then taken away. Questions about the picture test your ability to observe both details and larger elements.

5) Following directions

In many positions in the public service, the employee must be able to carry out written instructions dependably and accurately. You may be given a chart with several columns, each column listing a variety of information. The questions require you to carry out directions involving the information given in the chart.

6) Skills and aptitudes

Performance tests effectively measure some manual skills and aptitudes. When the skill is one in which you are trained, such as typing or shorthand, you can practice. These tests are often very much like those given in business school or high school courses. For many of the other skills and aptitudes, however, no short-time preparation can be made. Skills and abilities natural to you or that you have developed throughout your lifetime are being tested.

Many of the general questions just described provide all the data needed to answer the questions and ask you to use your reasoning ability to find the answers. Your best preparation for these tests, as well as for tests of facts and ideas, is to be at your physical and mental best. You, no doubt, have your own methods of getting into an exam-taking mood and keeping "in shape." The next section lists some ideas on this subject.

IV. KINDS OF QUESTIONS

Only rarely is the "essay" question, which you answer in narrative form, used in civil service tests. Civil service tests are usually of the short-answer type. Full instructions for answering these questions will be given to you at the examination. But in case this is your first experience with short-answer questions and separate answer sheets, here is what you need to know:

1) Multiple-choice Questions

Most popular of the short-answer questions is the "multiple choice" or "best answer" question. It can be used, for example, to test for factual knowledge, ability to solve problems or judgment in meeting situations found at work.

A multiple-choice question is normally one of three types—

- It can begin with an incomplete statement followed by several possible endings. You are to find the one ending which *best* completes the statement, although some of the others may not be entirely wrong.
- It can also be a complete statement in the form of a question which is answered by choosing one of the statements listed.
- It can be in the form of a problem – again you select the best answer.

Here is an example of a multiple-choice question with a discussion which should give you some clues as to the method for choosing the right answer:

When an employee has a complaint about his assignment, the action which will *best* help him overcome his difficulty is to
- A. discuss his difficulty with his coworkers
- B. take the problem to the head of the organization
- C. take the problem to the person who gave him the assignment
- D. say nothing to anyone about his complaint

In answering this question, you should study each of the choices to find which is best. Consider choice "A" – Certainly an employee may discuss his complaint with fellow employees, but no change or improvement can result, and the complaint remains unresolved. Choice "B" is a poor choice since the head of the organization probably does not know what assignment you have been given, and taking your problem to him is known as "going over the head" of the supervisor. The supervisor, or person who made the assignment, is the person who can clarify it or correct any injustice. Choice "C" is, therefore, correct. To say nothing, as in choice "D," is unwise. Supervisors have and interest in knowing the problems employees are facing, and the employee is seeking a solution to his problem.

2) True/False Questions

The "true/false" or "right/wrong" form of question is sometimes used. Here a complete statement is given. Your job is to decide whether the statement is right or wrong.

SAMPLE: A roaming cell-phone call to a nearby city costs less than a non-roaming call to a distant city.

This statement is wrong, or false, since roaming calls are more expensive.
This is not a complete list of all possible question forms, although most of the others are variations of these common types. You will always get complete directions for

answering questions. Be sure you understand *how* to mark your answers – ask questions until you do.

V. RECORDING YOUR ANSWERS

Computer terminals are used more and more today for many different kinds of exams.

For an examination with very few applicants, you may be told to record your answers in the test booklet itself. Separate answer sheets are much more common. If this separate answer sheet is to be scored by machine – and this is often the case – it is highly important that you mark your answers correctly in order to get credit.

An electronic scoring machine is often used in civil service offices because of the speed with which papers can be scored. Machine-scored answer sheets must be marked with a pencil, which will be given to you. This pencil has a high graphite content which responds to the electronic scoring machine. As a matter of fact, stray dots may register as answers, so do not let your pencil rest on the answer sheet while you are pondering the correct answer. Also, if your pencil lead breaks or is otherwise defective, ask for another.

Since the answer sheet will be dropped in a slot in the scoring machine, be careful not to bend the corners or get the paper crumpled.

The answer sheet normally has five vertical columns of numbers, with 30 numbers to a column. These numbers correspond to the question numbers in your test booklet. After each number, going across the page are four or five pairs of dotted lines. These short dotted lines have small letters or numbers above them. The first two pairs may also have a "T" or "F" above the letters. This indicates that the first two pairs only are to be used if the questions are of the true-false type. If the questions are multiple choice, disregard the "T" and "F" and pay attention only to the small letters or numbers.

Answer your questions in the manner of the sample that follows:

32. The largest city in the United States is
     A. Washington, D.C.
     B. New York City
     C. Chicago
     D. Detroit
     E. San Francisco

1) Choose the answer you think is best. (New York City is the largest, so "B" is correct.)
2) Find the row of dotted lines numbered the same as the question you are answering. (Find row number 32)
3) Find the pair of dotted lines corresponding to the answer. (Find the pair of lines under the mark "B.")
4) Make a solid black mark between the dotted lines.

VI. BEFORE THE TEST

Common sense will help you find procedures to follow to get ready for an examination. Too many of us, however, overlook these sensible measures. Indeed, nervousness and fatigue have been found to be the most serious reasons why applicants fail to do their best on civil service tests. Here is a list of reminders:

- Begin your preparation early – Don't wait until the last minute to go scurrying around for books and materials or to find out what the position is all about.
- Prepare continuously – An hour a night for a week is better than an all-night cram session. This has been definitely established. What is more, a night a week for a month will return better dividends than crowding your study into a shorter period of time.
- Locate the place of the exam – You have been sent a notice telling you when and where to report for the examination. If the location is in a different town or otherwise unfamiliar to you, it would be well to inquire the best route and learn something about the building.
- Relax the night before the test – Allow your mind to rest. Do not study at all that night. Plan some mild recreation or diversion; then go to bed early and get a good night's sleep.
- Get up early enough to make a leisurely trip to the place for the test – This way unforeseen events, traffic snarls, unfamiliar buildings, etc. will not upset you.
- Dress comfortably – A written test is not a fashion show. You will be known by number and not by name, so wear something comfortable.
- Leave excess paraphernalia at home – Shopping bags and odd bundles will get in your way. You need bring only the items mentioned in the official notice you received; usually everything you need is provided. Do not bring reference books to the exam. They will only confuse those last minutes and be taken away from you when in the test room.
- Arrive somewhat ahead of time – If because of transportation schedules you must get there very early, bring a newspaper or magazine to take your mind off yourself while waiting.
- Locate the examination room – When you have found the proper room, you will be directed to the seat or part of the room where you will sit. Sometimes you are given a sheet of instructions to read while you are waiting. Do not fill out any forms until you are told to do so; just read them and be prepared.
- Relax and prepare to listen to the instructions
- If you have any physical problem that may keep you from doing your best, be sure to tell the test administrator. If you are sick or in poor health, you really cannot do your best on the exam. You can come back and take the test some other time.

VII. AT THE TEST

The day of the test is here and you have the test booklet in your hand. The temptation to get going is very strong. Caution! There is more to success than knowing the right answers. You must know how to identify your papers and understand variations in the type of short-answer question used in this particular examination. Follow these suggestions for maximum results from your efforts:

1) Cooperate with the monitor

The test administrator has a duty to create a situation in which you can be as much at ease as possible. He will give instructions, tell you when to begin, check to see that you are marking your answer sheet correctly, and so on. He is not there to guard you, although he will see that your competitors do not take unfair advantage. He wants to help you do your best.

2) Listen to all instructions

Don't jump the gun! Wait until you understand all directions. In most civil service tests you get more time than you need to answer the questions. So don't be in a hurry. Read each word of instructions until you clearly understand the meaning. Study the examples, listen to all announcements and follow directions. Ask questions if you do not understand what to do.

3) Identify your papers

Civil service exams are usually identified by number only. You will be assigned a number; you must not put your name on your test papers. Be sure to copy your number correctly. Since more than one exam may be given, copy your exact examination title.

4) Plan your time

Unless you are told that a test is a "speed" or "rate of work" test, speed itself is usually not important. Time enough to answer all the questions will be provided, but this does not mean that you have all day. An overall time limit has been set. Divide the total time (in minutes) by the number of questions to determine the approximate time you have for each question.

5) Do not linger over difficult questions

If you come across a difficult question, mark it with a paper clip (useful to have along) and come back to it when you have been through the booklet. One caution if you do this – be sure to skip a number on your answer sheet as well. Check often to be sure that you have not lost your place and that you are marking in the row numbered the same as the question you are answering.

6) Read the questions

Be sure you know what the question asks! Many capable people are unsuccessful because they failed to *read* the questions correctly.

7) Answer all questions

Unless you have been instructed that a penalty will be deducted for incorrect answers, it is better to guess than to omit a question.

8) Speed tests

It is often better NOT to guess on speed tests. It has been found that on timed tests people are tempted to spend the last few seconds before time is called in marking answers at random – without even reading them – in the hope of picking up a few extra points. To discourage this practice, the instructions may warn you that your score will be "corrected" for guessing. That is, a penalty will be applied. The incorrect answers will be deducted from the correct ones, or some other penalty formula will be used.

9) Review your answers

    If you finish before time is called, go back to the questions you guessed or omitted to give them further thought. Review other answers if you have time.

10) Return your test materials

    If you are ready to leave before others have finished or time is called, take ALL your materials to the monitor and leave quietly. Never take any test material with you. The monitor can discover whose papers are not complete, and taking a test booklet may be grounds for disqualification.

VIII. EXAMINATION TECHNIQUES

1) Read the general instructions carefully. These are usually printed on the first page of the exam booklet. As a rule, these instructions refer to the timing of the examination; the fact that you should not start work until the signal and must stop work at a signal, etc. If there are any *special* instructions, such as a choice of questions to be answered, make sure that you note this instruction carefully.

2) When you are ready to start work on the examination, that is as soon as the signal has been given, read the instructions to each question booklet, underline any key words or phrases, such as *least, best, outline, describe* and the like. In this way you will tend to answer as requested rather than discover on reviewing your paper that you *listed without describing*, that you selected the *worst* choice rather than the *best* choice, etc.

3) If the examination is of the objective or multiple-choice type – that is, each question will also give a series of possible answers: A, B, C or D, and you are called upon to select the best answer and write the letter next to that answer on your answer paper – it is advisable to start answering each question in turn. There may be anywhere from 50 to 100 such questions in the three or four hours allotted and you can see how much time would be taken if you read through all the questions before beginning to answer any. Furthermore, if you come across a question or group of questions which you know would be difficult to answer, it would undoubtedly affect your handling of all the other questions.

4) If the examination is of the essay type and contains but a few questions, it is a moot point as to whether you should read all the questions before starting to answer any one. Of course, if you are given a choice – say five out of seven and the like – then it is essential to read all the questions so you can eliminate the two that are most difficult. If, however, you are asked to answer all the questions, there may be danger in trying to answer the easiest one first because you may find that you will spend too much time on it. The best technique is to answer the first question, then proceed to the second, etc.

5) Time your answers. Before the exam begins, write down the time it started, then add the time allowed for the examination and write down the time it must be completed, then divide the time available somewhat as follows:

- If 3-1/2 hours are allowed, that would be 210 minutes. If you have 80 objective-type questions, that would be an average of 2-1/2 minutes per question. Allow yourself no more than 2 minutes per question, or a total of 160 minutes, which will permit about 50 minutes to review.
- If for the time allotment of 210 minutes there are 7 essay questions to answer, that would average about 30 minutes a question. Give yourself only 25 minutes per question so that you have about 35 minutes to review.

6) The most important instruction is to *read each question* and make sure you know what is wanted. The second most important instruction is to *time yourself properly* so that you answer every question. The third most important instruction is to *answer every question*. Guess if you have to but include something for each question. Remember that you will receive no credit for a blank and will probably receive some credit if you write something in answer to an essay question. If you guess a letter – say "B" for a multiple-choice question – you may have guessed right. If you leave a blank as an answer to a multiple-choice question, the examiners may respect your feelings but it will not add a point to your score. Some exams may penalize you for wrong answers, so in such cases *only*, you may not want to guess unless you have some basis for your answer.

7) Suggestions
   a. Objective-type questions
      1. Examine the question booklet for proper sequence of pages and questions
      2. Read all instructions carefully
      3. Skip any question which seems too difficult; return to it after all other questions have been answered
      4. Apportion your time properly; do not spend too much time on any single question or group of questions
      5. Note and underline key words – *all, most, fewest, least, best, worst, same, opposite,* etc.
      6. Pay particular attention to negatives
      7. Note unusual option, e.g., unduly long, short, complex, different or similar in content to the body of the question
      8. Observe the use of "hedging" words – *probably, may, most likely,* etc.
      9. Make sure that your answer is put next to the same number as the question
      10. Do not second-guess unless you have good reason to believe the second answer is definitely more correct
      11. Cross out original answer if you decide another answer is more accurate; do not erase until you are ready to hand your paper in
      12. Answer all questions; guess unless instructed otherwise
      13. Leave time for review

   b. Essay questions
      1. Read each question carefully
      2. Determine exactly what is wanted. Underline key words or phrases.
      3. Decide on outline or paragraph answer

4. Include many different points and elements unless asked to develop any one or two points or elements
5. Show impartiality by giving pros and cons unless directed to select one side only
6. Make and write down any assumptions you find necessary to answer the questions
7. Watch your English, grammar, punctuation and choice of words
8. Time your answers; don't crowd material

8) Answering the essay question

Most essay questions can be answered by framing the specific response around several key words or ideas. Here are a few such key words or ideas:

M's: manpower, materials, methods, money, management
P's: purpose, program, policy, plan, procedure, practice, problems, pitfalls, personnel, public relations
   a. Six basic steps in handling problems:
      1. Preliminary plan and background development
      2. Collect information, data and facts
      3. Analyze and interpret information, data and facts
      4. Analyze and develop solutions as well as make recommendations
      5. Prepare report and sell recommendations
      6. Install recommendations and follow up effectiveness

   b. Pitfalls to avoid
      1. *Taking things for granted* – A statement of the situation does not necessarily imply that each of the elements is necessarily true; for example, a complaint may be invalid and biased so that all that can be taken for granted is that a complaint has been registered
      2. *Considering only one side of a situation* – Wherever possible, indicate several alternatives and then point out the reasons you selected the best one
      3. *Failing to indicate follow up* – Whenever your answer indicates action on your part, make certain that you will take proper follow-up action to see how successful your recommendations, procedures or actions turn out to be
      4. *Taking too long in answering any single question* – Remember to time your answers properly

IX. AFTER THE TEST

Scoring procedures differ in detail among civil service jurisdictions although the general principles are the same. Whether the papers are hand-scored or graded by machine we have described, they are nearly always graded by number. That is, the person who marks the paper knows only the number – never the name – of the applicant. Not until all the papers have been graded will they be matched with names. If other tests, such as training and experience or oral interview ratings have been given, scores will be combined. Different parts of the examination usually have different weights. For example, the written test might count 60 percent of the final grade, and a rating of training and experience 40 percent. In many jurisdictions, veterans will have a certain number of points added to their grades.

After the final grade has been determined, the names are placed in grade order and an eligible list is established. There are various methods for resolving ties between those who get the same final grade – probably the most common is to place first the name of the person whose application was received first. Job offers are made from the eligible list in the order the names appear on it. You will be notified of your grade and your rank as soon as all these computations have been made. This will be done as rapidly as possible.

People who are found to meet the requirements in the announcement are called "eligibles." Their names are put on a list of eligible candidates. An eligible's chances of getting a job depend on how high he stands on this list and how fast agencies are filling jobs from the list.

When a job is to be filled from a list of eligibles, the agency asks for the names of people on the list of eligibles for that job. When the civil service commission receives this request, it sends to the agency the names of the three people highest on this list. Or, if the job to be filled has specialized requirements, the office sends the agency the names of the top three persons who meet these requirements from the general list.

The appointing officer makes a choice from among the three people whose names were sent to him. If the selected person accepts the appointment, the names of the others are put back on the list to be considered for future openings.

That is the rule in hiring from all kinds of eligible lists, whether they are for typist, carpenter, chemist, or something else. For every vacancy, the appointing officer has his choice of any one of the top three eligibles on the list. This explains why the person whose name is on top of the list sometimes does not get an appointment when some of the persons lower on the list do. If the appointing officer chooses the second or third eligible, the No. 1 eligible does not get a job at once, but stays on the list until he is appointed or the list is terminated.

X. HOW TO PASS THE INTERVIEW TEST

The examination for which you applied requires an oral interview test. You have already taken the written test and you are now being called for the interview test – the final part of the formal examination.

You may think that it is not possible to prepare for an interview test and that there are no procedures to follow during an interview. Our purpose is to point out some things you can do in advance that will help you and some good rules to follow and pitfalls to avoid while you are being interviewed.

What is an interview supposed to test?

The written examination is designed to test the technical knowledge and competence of the candidate; the oral is designed to evaluate intangible qualities, not readily measured otherwise, and to establish a list showing the relative fitness of each candidate – as measured against his competitors – for the position sought. Scoring is not on the basis of "right" and "wrong," but on a sliding scale of values ranging from "not passable" to "outstanding." As a matter of fact, it is possible to achieve a relatively low score without a single "incorrect" answer because of evident weakness in the qualities being measured.

Occasionally, an examination may consist entirely of an oral test – either an individual or a group oral. In such cases, information is sought concerning the technical knowledges and abilities of the candidate, since there has been no written examination for this purpose. More commonly, however, an oral test is used to supplement a written examination.

Who conducts interviews?

The composition of oral boards varies among different jurisdictions. In nearly all, a representative of the personnel department serves as chairman. One of the members of the board may be a representative of the department in which the candidate would work. In some cases, "outside experts" are used, and, frequently, a businessman or some other representative of the general public is asked to serve. Labor and management or other special groups may be represented. The aim is to secure the services of experts in the appropriate field.

However the board is composed, it is a good idea (and not at all improper or unethical) to ascertain in advance of the interview who the members are and what groups they represent. When you are introduced to them, you will have some idea of their backgrounds and interests, and at least you will not stutter and stammer over their names.

What should be done before the interview?

While knowledge about the board members is useful and takes some of the surprise element out of the interview, there is other preparation which is more substantive. It *is* possible to prepare for an oral interview – in several ways:

1) Keep a copy of your application and review it carefully before the interview

This may be the only document before the oral board, and the starting point of the interview. Know what education and experience you have listed there, and the sequence and dates of all of it. Sometimes the board will ask you to review the highlights of your experience for them; you should not have to hem and haw doing it.

2) Study the class specification and the examination announcement

Usually, the oral board has one or both of these to guide them. The qualities, characteristics or knowledges required by the position sought are stated in these documents. They offer valuable clues as to the nature of the oral interview. For example, if the job involves supervisory responsibilities, the announcement will usually indicate that knowledge of modern supervisory methods and the qualifications of the candidate as a supervisor will be tested. If so, you can expect such questions, frequently in the form of a hypothetical situation which you are expected to solve. NEVER go into an oral without knowledge of the duties and responsibilities of the job you seek.

3) Think through each qualification required

Try to visualize the kind of questions you would ask if you were a board member. How well could you answer them? Try especially to appraise your own knowledge and background in each area, *measured against the job sought*, and identify any areas in which you are weak. Be critical and realistic – do not flatter yourself.

4) Do some general reading in areas in which you feel you may be weak

For example, if the job involves supervision and your past experience has NOT, some general reading in supervisory methods and practices, particularly in the field of human relations, might be useful. Do NOT study agency procedures or detailed manuals. The oral board will be testing your understanding and capacity, not your memory.

5) Get a good night's sleep and watch your general health and mental attitude

You will want a clear head at the interview. Take care of a cold or any other minor ailment, and of course, no hangovers.

What should be done on the day of the interview?

Now comes the day of the interview itself. Give yourself plenty of time to get there. Plan to arrive somewhat ahead of the scheduled time, particularly if your appointment is in the fore part of the day. If a previous candidate fails to appear, the board might be ready for you a bit early. By early afternoon an oral board is almost invariably behind schedule if there are many candidates, and you may have to wait. Take along a book or magazine to read, or your application to review, but leave any extraneous material in the waiting room when you go in for your interview. In any event, relax and compose yourself.

The matter of dress is important. The board is forming impressions about you – from your experience, your manners, your attitude, and your appearance. Give your personal appearance careful attention. Dress your best, but not your flashiest. Choose conservative, appropriate clothing, and be sure it is immaculate. This is a business interview, and your appearance should indicate that you regard it as such. Besides, being well groomed and properly dressed will help boost your confidence.

Sooner or later, someone will call your name and escort you into the interview room. *This is it.* From here on you are on your own. It is too late for any more preparation. But remember, you asked for this opportunity to prove your fitness, and you are here because your request was granted.

What happens when you go in?

The usual sequence of events will be as follows: The clerk (who is often the board stenographer) will introduce you to the chairman of the oral board, who will introduce you to the other members of the board. Acknowledge the introductions before you sit down. Do not be surprised if you find a microphone facing you or a stenotypist sitting by. Oral interviews are usually recorded in the event of an appeal or other review.

Usually the chairman of the board will open the interview by reviewing the highlights of your education and work experience from your application – primarily for the benefit of the other members of the board, as well as to get the material into the record. Do not interrupt or comment unless there is an error or significant misinterpretation; if that is the case, do not hesitate. But do not quibble about insignificant matters. Also, he will usually ask you some question about your education, experience or your present job – partly to get you to start talking and to establish the interviewing "rapport." He may start the actual questioning, or turn it over to one of the other members. Frequently, each member undertakes the questioning on a particular area, one in which he is perhaps most competent, so you can expect each member to participate in the examination. Because time is limited, you may also expect some rather abrupt switches in the direction the questioning takes, so do not be upset by it. Normally, a board member will not pursue a single line of questioning unless he discovers a particular strength or weakness.

After each member has participated, the chairman will usually ask whether any member has any further questions, then will ask you if you have anything you wish to add. Unless you are expecting this question, it may floor you. Worse, it may start you off on an extended, extemporaneous speech. The board is not usually seeking more information. The question is principally to offer you a last opportunity to present further qualifications or to indicate that you have nothing to add. So, if you feel that a significant qualification or characteristic has been overlooked, it is proper to point it out in a sentence or so. Do not compliment the board on the thoroughness of their examination – they have been sketchy, and you know it. If you wish, merely say, "No thank you, I have nothing further to add." This is a point where you can "talk yourself out" of a good impression or fail to present an important bit of information. Remember, *you close the interview yourself.*

The chairman will then say, "That is all, Mr. _____, thank you." Do not be startled; the interview is over, and quicker than you think. Thank him, gather your belongings and take your leave. Save your sigh of relief for the other side of the door.

How to put your best foot forward

Throughout this entire process, you may feel that the board individually and collectively is trying to pierce your defenses, seek out your hidden weaknesses and embarrass and confuse you. Actually, this is not true. They are obliged to make an appraisal of your qualifications for the job you are seeking, and they want to see you in your best light. Remember, they must interview all candidates and a non-cooperative candidate may become a failure in spite of their best efforts to bring out his qualifications. Here are 15 suggestions that will help you:

1) Be natural – Keep your attitude confident, not cocky

If you are not confident that you can do the job, do not expect the board to be. Do not apologize for your weaknesses, try to bring out your strong points. The board is interested in a positive, not negative, presentation. Cockiness will antagonize any board member and make him wonder if you are covering up a weakness by a false show of strength.

2) Get comfortable, but don't lounge or sprawl

Sit erectly but not stiffly. A careless posture may lead the board to conclude that you are careless in other things, or at least that you are not impressed by the importance of the occasion. Either conclusion is natural, even if incorrect. Do not fuss with your clothing, a pencil or an ashtray. Your hands may occasionally be useful to emphasize a point; do not let them become a point of distraction.

3) Do not wisecrack or make small talk

This is a serious situation, and your attitude should show that you consider it as such. Further, the time of the board is limited – they do not want to waste it, and neither should you.

4) Do not exaggerate your experience or abilities

In the first place, from information in the application or other interviews and sources, the board may know more about you than you think. Secondly, you probably will not get away with it. An experienced board is rather adept at spotting such a situation, so do not take the chance.

5) If you know a board member, do not make a point of it, yet do not hide it

Certainly you are not fooling him, and probably not the other members of the board. Do not try to take advantage of your acquaintanceship – it will probably do you little good.

6) Do not dominate the interview

Let the board do that. They will give you the clues – do not assume that you have to do all the talking. Realize that the board has a number of questions to ask you, and do not try to take up all the interview time by showing off your extensive knowledge of the answer to the first one.

7) Be attentive

You only have 20 minutes or so, and you should keep your attention at its sharpest throughout. When a member is addressing a problem or question to you, give him your undivided attention. Address your reply principally to him, but do not exclude the other board members.

8) Do not interrupt

A board member may be stating a problem for you to analyze. He will ask you a question when the time comes. Let him state the problem, and wait for the question.

9) Make sure you understand the question

Do not try to answer until you are sure what the question is. If it is not clear, restate it in your own words or ask the board member to clarify it for you. However, do not haggle about minor elements.

10) Reply promptly but not hastily

A common entry on oral board rating sheets is "candidate responded readily," or "candidate hesitated in replies." Respond as promptly and quickly as you can, but do not jump to a hasty, ill-considered answer.

11) Do not be peremptory in your answers

A brief answer is proper – but do not fire your answer back. That is a losing game from your point of view. The board member can probably ask questions much faster than you can answer them.

12) Do not try to create the answer you think the board member wants

He is interested in what kind of mind you have and how it works – not in playing games. Furthermore, he can usually spot this practice and will actually grade you down on it.

13) Do not switch sides in your reply merely to agree with a board member

Frequently, a member will take a contrary position merely to draw you out and to see if you are willing and able to defend your point of view. Do not start a debate, yet do not surrender a good position. If a position is worth taking, it is worth defending.

14) Do not be afraid to admit an error in judgment if you are shown to be wrong

The board knows that you are forced to reply without any opportunity for careful consideration. Your answer may be demonstrably wrong. If so, admit it and get on with the interview.

15) Do not dwell at length on your present job

The opening question may relate to your present assignment. Answer the question but do not go into an extended discussion. You are being examined for a *new* job, not your present one. As a matter of fact, try to phrase ALL your answers in terms of the job for which you are being examined.

Basis of Rating

Probably you will forget most of these "do's" and "don'ts" when you walk into the oral interview room. Even remembering them all will not ensure you a passing grade. Perhaps you did not have the qualifications in the first place. But remembering them will help you to put your best foot forward, without treading on the toes of the board members.

Rumor and popular opinion to the contrary notwithstanding, an oral board wants you to make the best appearance possible. They know you are under pressure – but they also want to see how you respond to it as a guide to what your reaction would be under the pressures of the job you seek. They will be influenced by the degree of poise you display, the personal traits you show and the manner in which you respond.

ABOUT THIS BOOK

This book contains tests divided into Examination Sections. Go through each test, answering every question in the margin. At the end of each test look at the answer key and check your answers. On the ones you got wrong, look at the right answer choice and learn. Do not fill in the answers first. Do not memorize the questions and answers, but understand the answer and principles involved. On your test, the questions will likely be different from the samples. Questions are changed and new ones added. If you understand these past questions you should have success with any changes that arise. Tests may consist of several types of questions. We have additional books on each subject should more study be advisable or necessary for you. Finally, the more you study, the better prepared you will be. This book is intended to be the last thing you study before you walk into the examination room. Prior study of relevant texts is also recommended. NLC publishes some of these in our Fundamental Series. Knowledge and good sense are important factors in passing your exam. Good luck also helps. So now study this Passbook, absorb the material contained within and take that knowledge into the examination. Then do your best to pass that exam.

―――――

EXAMINATION SECTION

EXAMINATION SECTION
TEST 1

DIRECTIONS: Each question or incomplete statement is followed by several suggested answers or completions. Select the l one that BEST answers the question or completes the statement. *PRINT THE LETTER OF THE CORRECT ANSWER IN THE SPACE AT THE RIGHT.*

1. The applicant you are interviewing is a man in his late forties who has recently lost his job and has a family of eight to support. He is very upset and tells you he does not know where he will get the money to purchase food for the family and pay the rent. He does not know what he will do if he is found not eligible for public assistance. He asks you whether you think he will be eligible. You feel the applicant has a good chance, and you think he should receive financial assistance, but you are not completely certain that he is eligible for public assistance under departmental policy.
Of the following, the BEST action for you to take is to

    A. reassure the applicant and tell him you are sure everything will be all right because there is no sense in worrying him before you know for certain that he is not eligible
    B. tell the applicant that as far as you are concerned he should receive public assistance but that you are not certain the department will go along with your recommendation
    C. tell the applicant that you are not sure that he will be found eligible for public assistance
    D. adopt a cool manner and tell the applicant that he must behave like an adult and not allow himself to become emotional about the situation

1.____

2. When conducting an interview with a client receiving public assistance, it would be LEAST important for you to try to

    A. understand the reasons for the client's statements
    B. conduct the interview on the client's intellectual level
    C. imitate the client's speech as much as possible
    D. impress the client with the agency's concern for his welfare

2.____

Questions 3-6.

DIRECTIONS: Questions 3 through 6 are to be answered SOLELY on basis of the following case history of the Foster family.

FOSTER CASE HISTORY

Form W-341-C	Date: Jan. 25, 2015
Rev. 3/1/03	Case Name: Foster
600M-804077-S-200 (93)-245	Case No. : ADC-3415968

Family Composition: Ann Foster, b. 7.23.77
Gerry   b. 1.7.02
Susan   b. 4.1.04
John   b. 5.3.07
Joan   b. 10.14.10

Mrs. Foster was widowed in June 2011 when her husband was killed in a car accident. Since that time, the family has received public assistance. Mrs. Foster has been referred for housekeeping service by the Social Service Department of Lincoln Hospital, where she is being treated in the neurology clinic. Her primary diagnosis is multiple sclerosis. The hospital reports that she is going through a period of deterioration characterized by an unsteady gait, and weakness and tremor in the limbs. At this time, her capacity to manage a household and four children is severely limited. She feels quite overwhelmed and is unable to function adequately in taking care of her home.

In addition to the medical reasons, it is advisable that a housekeeper be placed in the home as part of a total plan to avoid further family breakdown and deterioration. This deterioration is reflected by all family members. Mrs. Foster is severely depressed and is unable to meet the needs of her children, who have a variety of problems. Joan, the youngest, is not speaking, is hyperactive, and in general is not developing normally for a child her age. John is showing learning problems in school and has poor articulation. Susan was not promoted last year and is a behavior problem at home. Gerry, the oldest, is deformed due to a fire at age two. It is clear that Mrs. Foster cannot control or properly discipline her children, but even more important is the fact that she is unable to offer them the encouragement and guidance they require.

It is hoped that providing housekeeping service will relieve Mrs. Foster of the basic household chores so that she will be less frustrated and better able to provide the love and guidance needed by her children.

3. The age of the child who is described as not developing normally, hyperactive, and not speaking is

     A. 4   B. 7   C. 10   D. 13

3.____

4. Which of the following CANNOT be verified on the basis of the Foster Case History above?

     A. William Foster was Ann Foster's husband.
     B. Mrs. Foster has been seen in the neurology clinic at Lincoln Hospital.
     C. John Foster has trouble with his speech.
     D. The Foster family has received public assistance since June 2011.

4.____

5. The form on which the information about the Foster family is presented is known as

     A. Family Composition Form   B. Form Rev. 3/1/03
     C. Form W-341-C   D. ADC-3415968

5.____

6. According to the above case history, housekeeping service is being requested PRIMA-RILY because   6.____

  A. no one in the family can perform the household chores
  B. Mrs. Foster suffers from multiple sclerosis and requires assistance with the house-hold chores
  C. the children are exhibiting behavior problems resulti from the mother's illness
  D. the children have no father

7. You notice that an applicant whom you rejected for public assistance is back at the center the following morning and is waiting to be interviewed by another worker in your group. Of the following, the BEST approach for you to take is to 7.____

  A. inform the worker, before she interviews the applicant that you had interviewed and rejected him the previous day
  B. not inform the worker about the situation and let her make her own decision
  C. approach the applicant and tell him he was rejected for good reason and will have to leave the center immediately
  D. ask the special officer at the center to remove the applicant

8. You have just finished interviewing an applicant who has a violent temper and has dis-played a great amount of hostility toward you during the interview. You find he is ineligible for public assistance. Departmental policy is that all applicants are notified by mail in a day or so of their acceptance or rejection for public assistance. However, you also have the option, if you think it is desirable, of notifying the applicant at the interview. Of the following, the BEST action for you to take in this case is to 8.____

  A. tell the applicant of his rejection during the interview
  B. have the applicant notified of the results of the interview by mail only
  C. ask your supervisor to inform the applicant of his rejection
  D. inform the applicant of the results of the interview, with a special patrolman at your side

9. You are interviewing a client who speaks English poorly and whose native language is Spanish. Your knowledge of Spanish is very limited. Of the following, the FIRST action it would be best for you to take is to 9.____

  A. try to locate a worker at the center who speaks Spanish
  B. write our your questions because it is easier for people to understand a new lan-guage when it is written rather than when it is spoken
  C. do the best you can, using hand gestures to make yourself understood
  D. tell the client to return with a friend or relative who speaks English

10. During an interview with a client of another race, he accuses you of racial prejudice and asks for an interviewer of his own race. Of the following, which is the BEST way to handle the situation? 10.____

  A. In a friendly manner, tell the client that eligibility is based on the regulations and the facts, not on prejudice, and ask him to continue with the interview.
  B. Explain to your supervisor that you cannot deal with someone who accuses you of prejudice, and ask your supervisor to assign the client someone of his own race.
  C. Assure the client that you will lean over backwards to treat his application favorably.

D.   Tell the client that some of your friends are of his race and that you could therefore not possibly be prejudiced.

Questions 11-15.

DIRECTIONS: In order to answer Questions 11 through 15, assume that you have been asked to write a short report on the basis of the information contained in the following passage about the granting of emergency funds to the Smith family.

Mr. and Mrs. Smith, who have been receiving public assistance for the last six months, arrive at the center the morning of August 2, totally upset and anxious because they and their family have been burned out of their apartment the night before. The fire seems to have been of suspicious origin because at the time it broke out witnesses spotted two neighborhood teenagers running away from the scene. The policemen, who arrived at the scene shortly after the firemen, took down the pertinent information about the alleged arsonists.

The Smiths have spent the night with friends but now request emergency housing and emergency funds for themselves and their four children to purchase food and to replace the clothing which was destroyed by the fire. The burned-out apartment had consisted of 5 rooms and a bath, and the Smiths are now worried that they will be forced to accept smaller accommodations. Furthermore, since Mrs. Smith suffers from a heart murmur, she is worried that their new living quarters will necessitate her climbing too many stairs. Her previous apartment was a one-flight walk-up, which was acceptable.

As the worker in charge, you have studied the case, determined the amount of the emergency grant, made temporary arrangements for the Smiths to stay at a hotel, and reassured Mrs. Smith that everything possible will be done to find them an apartment which will meet with their approval.

11.   Which of the following would it be BEST to include in the report as the reason for the emergency grant?   11.____

A.   The police have decided that the fire is of suspicious origin.
B.   Two neighborhood teenagers were seen leaving the fire at the Smiths'.
C.   The apartment of the Smith family has been destroyed by fire.
D.   Mrs. Smith suffers from a heart murmur and cannot climb stairs.

12.   Which of the following would it be BEST to accept as verification of the fire?   12.____
A

A.,   letter from the friends with whom the Smiths stayed the previous night
B.   photograph of the fire
C.   dated newspaper clipping describing the fire
D.   note from the Smiths' neighbors

13.   A report of the Smith family's need for a new apartment must be sent to the center's housing specialist.   13.____
Which of the following recommendations for housing would be MOST appropriate?

A.   Two bedrooms, first floor walk-up
B.   Five rooms, ground floor
C.   Two-room suite, hotel with elevator
D.   Three rooms, building with elevator

14. For which of the following are the Smiths requesting emergency funds? 14._____

    A. Furniture
    B. Food
    C. A hotel room
    D. Repairs in their apartment

15. Which of the following statements provides the BEST summary of the action taken by you on the Smith case and is MOST important for inclusion in your report? 15._____

    A. Mr. and Mrs. Smith arrived upset and anxious and were reassured.
    B. It was verified that there was a fire.
    C. Temporary living arrangements were made, and the amount of the emergency grant was determined.
    D. The case was studied and a new apartment was found for the Smiths which met with their approval.

16. It is important that you remember what has happened between you and a client during an interview so that you may deliver appropriate services.
However, the one of the following which is the MOST likely reason that taking notes during the interview may not always be a good practice is that 16._____

    A. you may lose the notes and have to go back and see the client again
    B. some clients may believe that you are not interested in what they are saying
    C. you are the only one who is likely to read the notes
    D. some clients may believe that you are not smart enough to remember what happened in the interview

17. Before an applicant seeking public assistance can be interviewed, he must fill out a complex application form which consists of eleven pages of questions requesting very detailed information.
Of the following, the BEST time for you to review the information on the application form is 17._____

    A. before she begins to interview the applicant
    B. after she has asked the applicant a few questions to put him at ease
    C. towards the end of the interview so that she has a chance to think about the information received during the interview
    D. after the interview has been completed

Questions 18-20.

DIRECTIONS: In Questions 18 through 20, choose the lettered word which means MOST NEARLY the same as the underlined word in the sentence.

18. He needed public assistance because he was incapacitated. The word incapacitated means MOST NEARLY 18._____

    A. uneducated
    B. disabled
    C. uncooperative
    D. discharged

19. The caseworker explained to the client that signing the document was compulsory. The word compulsory means MOST NEARLY 19._____

    A. temporary
    B. required
    C. different
    D. comprehensive

20. The woman's actions did not <u>jeopardize</u> her eligibility for benefits.   20._____
The word <u>jeopardize</u> means MOST NEARLY

   A. delay   B. reinforce   C. determine   D. endanger

KEY (CORRECT ANSWERS)

1.	C	11.	C
2.	C	12.	C
3.	A	13.	B
4.	A	14.	B
5.	C	15.	C
6.	B	16.	B
7.	A	17.	A
8.	B	18.	B
9.	A	19.	B
10.	A	20.	D

TEST 2

DIRECTIONS: Each question or incomplete statement is followed by several suggested answers or completions. Select the one that BEST answers the question or completes the statement. *PRINT THE LETTER OF THE CORRECT ANSWER IN THE SPACE AT THE RIGHT.*

Questions 1-4.

DIRECTIONS: Questions 1 through 4 are to be answered on the basis of the information given in the Fact Situation and Sample Form below.

FACT SITUATION

On October 7, 2014, John Smith (Case #ADC-U 1467912) applied and was accepted for public assistance for himself and his family. His family consists of his wife, Helen, and their children: William, age 9; John Jr., age 6; and Mary, age 2. The family has lived in a five-room apartment located at 142 West 137 Street, Manhattan, since July 18, 2008. Mr. Smith signed a 2-year lease for this apartment on July 18, 2014 at a rent of $500 per month. The maximum rental allowance for a family of this size is $420 per month. Utilities are included in this rent-controlled multiple dwelling.

Since the cost of renting this apartment is in excess of the allowable amount, the Supervising Clerk (Income Maintenance) is required to fill out a "Request for Approval of Exception to Policy for Shelter Allowance/Rehousing Expenses."

A sample of a section of this form follows.

SAMPLE FORM

REQUEST FOR APPROVAL OF EXCEPTION TO POLICY FOR SHELTER ALLOWANCE /REHOUSING EXPENSES

Case Name	Case No. or Pending		Acceptance Date	Group No.	
Present ZIP Address	Apt. No. or Location	No. of Rooms	Rent per Mo. $	Occupancy Date	
HOUSEHOLD COMPOSITION (List all persons living in the household) Column I Surname First	Col. 2 Birth-date	Col. 3 Sex	Column 4 Relation to Case Head	Column 5 Marital Status	Column 6 P. A. Status

1. Based on the information given in the Fact Situation, which one of the following should be entered in the space for *Occupancy Date?*   1.____

   A. October 7, 2014
   B. July 18, 2014
   C. July 18, 2008
   D. Unknown

2. What amount should be entered in the space labeled *Rent per Mo.* ?   2.____

   A. $500   B. $420   C. $300   D. $80

3. Based on the information given in the Fact Situation, it is IMPOSSIBLE to fill in which one of the following blanks?   3.____

   A. *Case Number or pending*
   B. *Acceptance Date*
   C. *Apt. No. or Location*
   D. *No. of Rooms*

4. Which of the following should be entered in Column 4 for Helen Smith?   4.____

   A. Wife   B. Head   C. Mother   D. Unknown

Questions 5-13.

DIRECTIONS: In Questions 5 through 13, perform the computations indicated and choose the CORRECT answer from the four choices given.

5. Add $4.34, $34.50, $6.00, $101.76, $90.67. From the result, subtract $60.54 and $10.56.   5.____

   A. $76.17   B. $156.37   C. $166.17   D. $300.37

6. Add 2,200, 2,600, 252, and 47.96.
   From the result, subtract 202.70, 1,200, 2,150, and 434.43.   6.____

   A. 1,112.83   B. 1,213.46   C. 1,341.51   D. 1,348.91

7. Multiply 1850 by .05 and multiply 3300 by .08 and then add both results.   7.____

   A. 242.50   B. 264.00   C. 333.25   D. 356.50

8. Multiply 312.77 by .04.
   Round off the result to the nearest hundredth.   8.____

   A. 12.52   B. 12.511   C. 12.518   D. 12.51

9. Add 362.05, 91.13, 347.81, and 17.46, and then divide the result by 6.
   The answer rounded off to the nearest hundredth is   9.____

   A. 138.409   B. 137.409   C. 136.41   D. 136.40

10. Add 66.25 and 15.06, and then multiply the result by 2 1/6.
    The answer is MOST NEARLY   10.____

   A. 176.18   B. 176.17   C. 162.66   D. 162.62

11. Each of the following options contains three decimals. In which case do all three decimals have the same value?   11.____

   A. .3; .30; .03
   B. .25; .250; .2500
   C. 1.9; 1.90; 1.09
   D. .35; .350; .035

8

12. Add 1/2 the sum of (539.84 and 479.26) to 1/3 the sum of (1461.93 and 927.27). Round off the result to the nearest whole number.

    A. 3408   B. 2899   C. 1816   D. 1306

12.____

13. Multiply $5,906.09 by 15%, and then divide the result by 1/3.

    A. $295.30   B. $885.91   C. $8,859.14   D. $29,530.45

13.____

Questions 14-18.

DIRECTIONS: Questions 14 through 18 are to be answered SOLELY on the basis of the information provided in the following passage.

The ideal relationship for the interview is one of mutual confidence. To try to pretend, to put on a front of cordiality and friendship is extremely unwise for the interviewer because he will certainly convey, by subtle means, his real feelings. It is the interviewer's responsibility to take the lead in establishing a relationship of mutual confidence.

As the interviewer, you should help the interviewee to feel at ease and ready to talk. One of the best ways to do this is to be at ease yourself. If you are, it will probably be evident; if you are not, it will almost certainly be apparent to the interviewee.

Begin the interview with topics for discussion which are easy to talk about and non-menacing. This interchange can be like the conversation of people when they are waiting for a bus, at the ball game, or discussing the weather. However, do not prolong this warm-up too long since the interviewee knows as well as you do that these are not the things he came to discuss. Delaying too long in getting down to business may suggest to him that you are reluctant to deal with the topic.

Once you get onto the main topics, do all that you can to get the interviewee to talk freely with as little prodding from you as possible. This will probably require that you give him some idea of the area, and of ways of looking at it. Avoid, however, prejudicing or coloring his remarks by what you say; especially, do not in any way indicate that there are certain things you want to hear, others which you do not want to hear. It is essential that he feel free to express his own ideas unhampered by your ideas, your values and preconceptions.

Do not appear to dominate the interview, nor have even the suggestion of a patronizing attitude. Ask some questions which will enable the interviewee to take pride in his knowledge. Take the attitude that the interviewee sincerely wants the interview to achieve its purpose. This creates a warm, permissive atmosphere that is most important in all interviews.

14. Of the following, the BEST title for the above passage is

    A. PERMISSIVENESS IN INTERVIEWING
    B. INTERVIEWING TECHNIQUES
    C. THE FACTOR OF PRETENSE IN THE INTERVIEW
    D. THE CORDIAL INTERVIEW

14.____

15. Which of the following recommendations on the conduct of an interview is made by the above passage?   15.____

    A. Conduct the interview as if it were an interchange between people discussing the weather.
    B. The interview should be conducted in a highly impersonal manner.
    C. Allow enough time for the interview so that the interviewee does not feel rushed.
    D. Start the interview with topics which are not threatening to the interviewee.

16. The above passage indicates that the interviewer should   16.____

    A. feel free to express his opinions
    B. patronize the interviewee and display a permissive attitude
    C. permit the interviewee to give the needed information in his own fashion
    D. provide for privacy when conducting the interview

17. The meaning of the word *unhampered,* as it is used in the last sentence of the fourth paragraph of the preceding passage, is MOST NEARLY   17.____

    A. unheeded
    B. unobstructed
    C. hindered
    D. aided

18. It can be INFERRED from the above passage that   18.____

    A. interviewers, while generally mature, lack confidence
    B. certain methods in interviewing are more successful than others in obtaining information
    C. there is usually a reluctance on the part of interviewers to deal with unpleasant topics
    D. it is best for the interviewer not to waiver from the use of hard and fast rules when dealing with clients

19. The applicant whom you are interviewing is not talking rationally, and he admits that he is under the influence of alcohol.
Which of the following is the BEST way of handling this situation?   19.____

    A. Call a security guard and have the applicant removed.
    B. Tell the applicant that unless he gets control of himself, he will not receive financial assistance.
    C. Send out for a cup of black coffee for the applicant.
    D. End the interview and plan to schedule another appointment.

20. During an interview, an applicant who has submitted an application for assistance breaks down and cries. Of the following, the BEST way of handling this situation is to   20.____

    A. end the interview and schedule a new appointment
    B. be patient and sympathetic, and encourage the applicant to continue the interview
    C. tell the applicant sternly that crying will not help matters
    D. tell the applicant that you will do everything you can to get the application approved

KEY (CORRECT ANSWERS)

1.	C		11.	B
2.	A		12.	D
3.	C		13.	A
4.	A		14.	B
5.	C		15.	D
6.	A		16.	C
7.	D		17.	B
8.	D		18.	B
9.	C		19.	D
10.	B		20.	B

EXAMINATION SECTION
TEST 1

DIRECTIONS: Each question or incomplete statement is followed by several suggested answers or completions. Select the one that BEST answers the question or completes the statement. *PRINT THE LETTER OF THE CORRECT ANSWER IN THE SPACE AT THE RIGHT.*

1. Assume that an applicant, obviously under a great deal of stress, talks continuously and rambles, making it difficult for you to determine the exact problem and her need. In order to make the interview more successful, it would be BEST for you to
    A. interrupt the applicant and ask her specific questions in order to get the information you need
    B. tell the applicant that her rambling may be a basic cause of her problem
    C. let the applicant continue talking as long as she wishes
    D. ask the applicant to get to the point because other people are waiting for you

1.____

2. A worker must be able to interview clients all day and still be able to listen and maintain interest.
Of the following, it is MOST important for you to show interest in the client because, if you appear interested,
    A. the client is more likely to appreciate your professional status
    B. the client is more likely to disclose a greater amount of information
    C. the client is less likely to tell lies
    D. you are more likely to gain your supervisor's approval

2.____

3. The application process is overwhelming to applicant Ms. M. She is very anxious and is fearful that she does not have all that she needs to be eligible for assistance. As a result, every time she is asked to produce a verifying document during the interview, she fumbles and drops all the other documents to the floor.
Of the following, the MOST effective method for you to use to complete the application process is to
    A. ask Ms. M not to be so nervous because you cannot get the work done if she fusses so much
    B. take the documents away from Ms. M and do it your self
    C. suggest that Ms. M get a friend to come and help her with the papers
    D. try to calm Ms. M and tell her that you are willing to help her with the papers to get the information you require

3.____

4. An applicant for public assistance claims that her husband deserted the family and that she needs money immediately for food since her children have not eaten for two days. Under normal procedure, she has to wait several days before she can be given any money for this purpose. In accordance with departmental policy, no exception can be made in this case.
Of the following, the BEST action for you to take is to
  A. tell her that, according to departmental policy, she cannot be given money immediately
  B. purchase some food for her, using your own funds, so that she can feed her children
  C. take up a collection among co-workers
  D. send her to another center

4.____

5. Applicants for public assistance often complain about the length of the application form. They also claim that the questions are too personal, since all they want is money. It is true that the form is long, but the answers to all the questions on the form are needed so that the department can make a decision on eligibility.
When applicants complain, which of the following would be the MOST appropriate action for you to take?
  A. Help such applicants understand that each question has a purpose which will help in the determination of eligibility
  B. Tell such applicants that you agree but that you must comply with regulations because it is your job
  C. Tell such applicants that they should stop complaining if they want you to help
  D. Refer such applicants to a supervisor who will explain agency policy

5.____

6. Which one of the following statements BEST describes the primary goal of a worker?
  A. Process as many clients in as short a time as possible
  B. Help his clients
  C. Grow into a more understanding person
  D. Assert his authority

6.____

7. Restating a question before the person being interviewed gives an answer to the original question is usually NOT good practice *principally* because
  A. the client will think that you don't know your job
  B. it may confuse the client
  C. the interviewer should know exactly what to ask and how to put the question
  D. it reveals the interviewer's insecurity

7.____

8. A white worker can BEST improve his ability to work with black clients if he
  A. tries to forget that the clients are black
  B. tells the black clients that he has no prejudices
  C. becomes aware of the problems black clients face
  D. socializes with black workers in the agency

8.____

9. A client warns that if he does not get what he wants he will report you to your supervisor and, if necessary, to the mayor's office.
    Of the following, the MOST appropriate response for you to make in this situation is to

    A. encourage the client to do as he threatens because you know that you are right
    B. call your supervisor in so that the client may confront him
    C. explain to the client how the decision will be made on his request and suggest what action he can take if there is an adverse decision
    D. try to understand the client's problem but tell him that he must not explode in the office because you will have to ask him to leave if he does

9.____

Questions 10-20.

DIRECTIONS: Refer to the following Semi-Monthly Family Allowance Schedule and Conversion Table when answering Questions 10 through 20.

SEMI-MONTHLY FAMILY ALLOWANCE SCHEDULE
(Based on Number of Persons in Household)

NUMBER OF PERSONS IN HOUSEHOLD						
One	Two	Three	Four	Five	Six	Each Additional Person
$470.00	$750.00	$1000.00	$1290.00	$1590.00	$1840.00	$25.00

CONVERSION TABLE - WEEKLY TO SEMI-MONTHLY AMOUNTS

DOLLARS				CENTS			
Weekly Amount	Semi-Monthly Amount	Weekly Amount	Semi-Monthly Amount	Weekly Amount	Semi-Monthly Amount	Weekly Amount	Semi-Monthly Amount
$10.00	$21.70	$510.00	$1105.00	$0.10	$0.20	$5.10	$11.10
20.00	43.30	520.00	1126.70	0.20	0.40	5.20	11.30
30.00	65.00	530.00	1148.30	0.30	0.70	5.30	11.50
40.00	86.70	540.00	1170.00	0.40	0.90	5.40	11.70
50.00	108.30	550.00	1191.70	0.50	1.10	5.50	11.90
60.00	130.00	560.00	1213.30	0.60	1.30	5.60	12.10
70.00	151.70	570.00	1235.00	0.70	1.50	5.70	12.40
80.00	173.30	580.00	1256.70	0.80	1.70	5.80	12.60
90.00	195.00	590.00	1278.30	0.90	2.00	5.90	12.80
100.00	216.70	600.00	1300.00	1.00	2.20	6.00	13.00
110.00	238.30	610.00	1321.70	1.10	2.40	6.10	13.20
120.00	260.00	620.00	1343.30	1.20	2.60	6.20	13.40
130.00	281.70	630.00	1365.00	1.30	2.80	6.30	13.70
140.00	303.30	640.00	1386.70	1.40	3.00	6.40	13.90
150.00	325.00	650.00	1408.30	1.50	3.30	6.50	14.10
160.00	346.70	660.00	1430.00	1.60	3.50	6.60	14.30
170.00	368.30	670.00	1451.70	1.70	3.70	6.70	14.50
180.00	390.00	680.00	1473.30	1.80	3.90	6.80	14.70
190.00	411.70	690.00	1495.00	1.90	4.10	6.90	15.00
200.00	433.30	700.00	1516.70	2.00	4.30	7.00	15.20
210.00	455.00	710.00	1538.30	2.10	4.60	7.10	15.40
220.00	476.70	720.00	1560.00	2.20	4.80	7.20	15.60
230.00	498.30	730.00	1581.70	2.30	5.00	7.30	15.80
240.00	520.00	740.00	1603.30	2.40	5.20	7.40	16.00
250.00	541.70	750.00	1625.00	2.50	5.40	7.50	16.30
260.00	563.30	760.00	1646.70	2.60	5.60	7.60	16.50
270.00	585.00	770.00	1668.30	2.70	5.90	7.70	16.70
280.00	606.70	780.00	1690.00	2.80	6.10	7.80	16.90
290.00	628.30	790.00	1711.70	2.90	6.30	7.90	17.10
300.00	650.00	800.00	1733.30	3.00	6.50	8.00	17.30
310.00	671.70	810.00	1755.00	3.10	6.70	8.10	17.60
320.00	693.30	820.00	1776.70	3.20	6.90	8.20	17.80
330.00	715.00	830.00	1798.30	3.30	7.20	8.30	18.00
340.00	736.70	840.00	1820.00	3.40	7.40	8.40	18.20
350.00	783.00	850.00	1841.70	3.50	7.60	8.50	18.40
360.00	780.00	860.00	1863.30	3.60	7.80	8.60	18.60
370.00	801.70	870.00	1885.00	3.70	8.00	8.70	18.90
380.00	823.30	880.00	1906.70	3.80	8.20	8.80	19.10
390.00	845.00	890.00	1928.30	3.90	8.50	8.90	18.30
400.00	866.70	900.00	1950.00	4.00	8.70	9.00	19.50
410.00	888.30	910.00	1971.70	4.10	8.90	9.10	19.70
420.00	910.00	920.00	1993.30	4.20	9.10	9.20	19.90
430.00	931.70	930.00	2015.00	4.30	9.30	9.30	20.20
440.00	953.30	940.00	2036.70	4.40	9.50	9.40	20.40
450.00	975.00	950.00	2058.30	4.50	9.80	9.50	20.60
460.00	996.70	960.00	2080.00	4.60	10.00	9.60	20.80
470.00	1018.30	970.00	2101.70	4.70	10.20	9.70	21.00
480.00	1040.00	980.00	2123.30	4.80	10.40	9.80	21.20
490.00	1061.70	990.00	2145.00	4.90	10.60	9.90	21.50
500.00	1083.30	1000.00	2166.70	5.00	10.80		

NOTE: Questions 10 through 20 are to be answered SOLELY on the basis of the Schedule and Table given above and the information and case situations given below.

Questions 10 through 14 are based on Case Situation #1.
Questions 15 through 20 are based on Case Situation #2.

Public assistance grants are computed on a semi-monthly basis. This means that all figures are first broken down into semi-monthly amounts, and that when a client receives a check twice a month, each semi-monthly check covers his requirements for a period of approximately 2-1/6 weeks. The grants are computed by means of the following procedures.

1. Determine the semi-monthly allowance for the family from the Semi-Monthly Family Allowance Schedule.
2. Determine total semi-monthly income by deducting from the semi-monthly gross earnings (the wages or salary *before* payroll deductions) all semi-monthly expenses for federal, state, and city income taxes, Social Security payments, State Disability Insurance payments, union dues, cost of transportation, and $10.00 per work day for lunch.
3. Add the semi-monthly allowance and the semi-monthly rent (monthly rent must be divided in half).
4. Subtract the semi-monthly income (if there is any income).
5. The formula for computing the semi-monthly grant is:
   Family Allowance + Rent (semi-monthly)

   | Total Income | (semi-monthly) |
   | = Amount of Grant | (semi-monthly) |
6. Refer to the Conversion Table in order to convert weekly amounts into semi-monthly amounts.

CASE SITUATION #1

The Smiths receive public assistance. The family includes John Smith, his wife Barbara, and their four children. They occupy a five-room apartment for which the rent is $1050.00 per month. Mr. Smith is employed as a cleaner and his gross wages are $1000 per week. He is employed 5 days a week and spends $7.00 a day carfare. He buys his lunches. The following weekly deductions are made from his salary:

Social Security	$60.00
Disability Benefits	3.80
Federal Income Tax	43.00
State Income Tax	28.00
City Income Tax	10.00

CASE SITUATION #2

The Jones family receives public assistance. The family includes Steven and Diane Jones and their two children. They occupy a four-room apartment for which the rental is $850.00 a month. Mr. Jones is employed as a handyman, and his gross wages are $900 per week. He is employed 4 days a week and spends $7.00 a day carfare. He buys his lunches. He has the following weekly deductions made from his salary:

Social Security	$40.00
Disability Benefits	2.70
Federal Income Tax	38.90
State Income Tax	20.50
City Income Tax	6.20

10. The weekly amount that Mr. Smith contributes towards Social Security, Disability Benefits, and income taxes is
    A. $313.70   B. $231.40   C. $144.80   D. $106.80   10.___

11. The semi-monthly family allowance for the Smith family is
    A. $1290.00   B. $1590.00   C. $1840.00   D. $1845.00   11.___

12. What is the total of semi-monthly expenses related to Mr. Smith's employment which will be deducted from semi-monthly gross earnings to compute semi-monthly income?
    A. $497.80   B. $422.00   C. $389.50   D. $229.80   12.___

13. Which of the following amounts is the total semi-monthly income for the Smith family?
    A. $2166.70   B. $2000.00   C. $1668.90   D. $1004.40   13.___

14. The amount of the grant which the Smith family is entitled to receive is
    A. $2365.00   B. $1840.00   C. $1392.20   D. $696.10   14.___

15. The weekly amount that Mr. Jones contributes towards Social Security, Disability Benefits, and income taxes is
    A. $108.30   B. $176.30   C. $234.30   D. $234.70   15.___

16. The semi-monthly family allowance for the Jones family is
    A. $750.00   B. $1000.00   C. $1220.00   D. $1290.00   16.___

17. The total of semi-monthly expenses related to Mr. Jones' employment which will be deducted from semi-monthly gross earnings is
    A. $172.30   B. $189.30   C. $382.00   D. $407.20   17.___

18. Which of the following amounts is the total semi-monthly income for the Jones family?   18.____
    A. $1282.00   B. $1553.20   C. $1568.00   D. $2122.30

19. The grant which the Jones family will receive is   19.____
    A. $147.00   B. $294.00   C. $1290.00   D. $1715.00

20. If Mrs. Jones' monthly rent had been $1050, what would the amount of the grant be?   20.____
    A. $247.00   B. $494.00   C. $772.00   D. $1822.00

KEY (CORRECT ANSWERS)

1.	A		11.	C
2.	B		12.	A
3.	D		13.	C
4.	A		14.	D
5.	A		15.	A
6.	B		16.	D
7.	B		17.	C
8.	C		18.	C
9.	C		19.	A
10.	C		20.	A

TEST 2

DIRECTIONS: Each question or incomplete statement is followed by several suggested answers or completions. Select the one that BEST answers the question or completes the statement. *PRINT THE LETTER OF THE CORRECT ANSWER IN THE SPACE AT THE RIGHT.*

Questions 1-5.

DIRECTIONS: Each of Questions 1 through 5 consists of information given in outline form and four sentences labeled A, B, C, and D. For each question, choose the one sentence which CORRECTLY expresses the information given in outline form and which also displays PROPER English usage.

1. Client's Name - Joanna Jones
    Number of Children - 3
    Client's Income - None
    Client's Marital Status - Single
    A. Joanna Jones is an unmarried client with three children who have no income.
    B. Joanna Jones, who is single and has no income, a client she has three children.
    C. Joanna Jones, whose three children are clients, is single and has no income.
    D. Joanna Jones, who has three children, is an unmarried client with no income.

1.____

2. Client's Name - Bertha Smith
    Number of Children - 2
    Client's Rent - $1050 per month
    Number of Rooms- 4
    A. Bertha Smith, a client, pays $1050 per month for her four rooms with two children.
    B. Client Bertha Smith has two children and pays $1050 per month for four rooms.
    C. Client Bertha Smith is paying $1050 per month for two children with four rooms.
    D. For four rooms and two children, Client Bertha Smith pays $1050 per month.

2.____

3. Name of Employee - Cynthia Dawes
    Number of Cases Assigned - 9
    Date Cases Were Assigned - 12/16
    Number of Assigned Cases Completed - 8
    A. On December 16, employee Cynthia Dawes was assigned nine cases; she has completed eight of these cases.
    B. Cynthia Dawes, employee on December 16, assigned nine cases, completed eight.
    C. Being employed on December 16, Cynthia Dawes completed eight of nine assigned cases.
    D. Employee Cynthia Dawes, she was assigned nine cases and completed eight, on December 16.

3.____

4. Place of Audit - Broadway Center
    Names of Auditors - Paul Cahn, Raymond Perez
    Date of Audit - 11/20
    Number of Cases Audited - 41
    A. On November 20, at the Broadway Center 41 cases was audited by auditors Paul Cahn and Raymond Perez.
    B. Auditors Raymond Perez and Paul Cahn has audited 41 cases at the Broadway

4.____

Center, on November 20.

C. At the Broadway Center, on November 20, auditors Paul Cahn and Raymond Perez audited 41 cases.
D. Auditors Paul Cahn and Raymond Perez at the Broadway Center, on November 20, is auditing 41 cases.

5. Name of Client - Barbra Levine   5._____
    Client's Monthly Income - $2100
    Client's Monthly Expenses - $4520
    A. Barbra Levine is a client, her monthly income is $2100 and her monthly expenses is $4520.
    B. Barbra Levine's monthly income is $2100 and she is a client, with whose monthly expenses are $4520.
    C. Barbra Levine is a client whose monthly income is $2100 and whose monthly expenses are $4520.
    D. Barbra Levine, a client, is with a monthly income which is $2100 and monthly expenses which are $4520.

Questions 6-10.

DIRECTIONS: Questions 6 through 10 are to be answered SOLELY on the basis of the information contained in the following passage.

Any person who is living in New York City and is otherwise eligible may be granted public assistance whether or not he has New York State residence. However, since New York City does not contribute to the cost of assistance granted to persons who are without State residence, the cases of all recipients must be formally identified as to whether or not each member of the household has State residence.

To acquire State residence a person must have resided in New York State continuously for one year. Such residence is not lost unless the person is out of the State continuously for a period of one year or longer. Continuous residence does not include any period during which the individual is a patient in a hospital, an inmate of a public institution or of an incorporated private institution, a resident on a military reservation or a minor residing in a boarding home while under the care of an authorized agency. Receipt of public assistance does not prevent a person from acquiring State residence. State residence, once acquired, is not lost because of absence from the State while a person is serving in the U.S. Armed Forces or the Merchant Marine; nor does a member of the family of such a person lose State residence while living with or near that person in these circumstances.

Each person, regardless of age, acquires or loses State residence as an individual. There is no derivative State residence except for an infant at the time of birth. He is deemed to have State residence if he is in the custody of both parents and either one of them has State residence, or if the parent having custody of him has State residence.

6. According to the above passage, an infant is deemed to have New York State residence at the time of his birth *if*
    A. he is born in New York State but neither of his parents is a resident
    B. he is in the custody of only one parent, who is not a resident, but his other parent is a resident
    C. his brother and sister are residents
    D. he is in the custody of both his parents but only one of them is a resident

6._____

7. The Jones family consists of five members. Jack and Mary Jones have lived in New York State continuously for the past eighteen months after having lived in Ohio since they were born. Of their three children, one was born ten months ago and has been in the custody of his parents since birth. Their second child lived in Ohio until six months ago and then moved in with his parents. Their third child had never lived in New York until he moved with his parents to New York eighteen months ago. However, he entered the armed forces one month later and has not lived in New York since that time.
Based on the above passage, how many members of the Jones family are New York State residents?
    A. 2   B. 3   C. 4   D. 5

7._____

8. Assuming that each of the following individuals has lived continuously in New York State for the past year, and has never previously lived in the State, which one of them is a New York State resident?
    A. Jack Salinas, who has been an inmate in a State correctional facility for six months of the year
    B. Fran Johnson, who has lived on an Army base for the entire year
    C. Arlene Snyder, who married a non-resident during the past year
    D. Gary Phillips, who was a patient in a Veterans Administration hospital for the entire year

8._____

9. The above passage implies that the reason for determining whether or not a recipient of public assistance is a State resident is that
    A. the cost of assistance for non-residents is not a New York City responsibility
    B. non-residents living in New York City are not eligible for public assistance
    C. recipients of public assistance are barred from acquiring State residence
    D. New York City is responsible for the full cost of assistance to recipients who are residents

9._____

10. Assume that the Rollins household in New York City consists of six members at the present time - Anne Rollins, her three children, her aunt and her uncle. Anne Rollins and one of her children moved to New York City seven months ago. Neither of them had previously lived in New York State. Her other two children have lived in New York City continuously for the past two years, as has her aunt. Anne Rollins' uncle had lived in New York City continuously for many years until two years ago. He then entered the armed forces and has returned to New York City within the past month.
Based on the above passage, how many members of the Rollins' household are New York State residents?
    A. 2   B. 3   C. 4   D. 6

10._____

11. You are interviewing a client to determine whether financial assistance should be continued and   11.____
    you find that what he is telling you does not agree exactly with your records.
    Of the following, the BEST way to handle this situation is to
    - A.   recommend that his public assistance payments be stopped, since you have
           caught him lying to you
    - B.   tell the client about the points of disagreement and ask him if he can clear them
           up
    - C.   give the client the benefit of the doubt and recommend continuation of his payments
    - D.   show the client the records and warn him that he must either tell the truth or lose
           his benefits

12. An applicant for public assistance gets angry at some of the questions you must ask her.   12.____
    Of the following, the BEST way to handle this situation is to
    - A.   assume that she is trying to hide something, and end the interview
    - B.   skip the questions that bother her and come back to them at the end of the interview
    - C.   tell her that she must either answer the question or leave
    - D.   explain to her that you are required to get answers to all the questions in order to be
           able to help her

13. At the end of an interview to determine whether financial assistance should be continued, the client   13.____
    offers to take you to lunch.
    Of the following, the BEST response to such an invitation is to
    - A.   tell the client that you do not take bribes and report the matter to your
           supervisor
    - B.   accept the invitation if you have the time, but do not let it influence your
           recommendation as to his eligibility for continuing public assistance
    - C.   politely refuse the invitation, and do not let it influence your
           recommendation as to his continuing eligibility for public assistance
    - D.   point out to the client that his budget does not include money for
           entertainment

Questions 14-18.

DIRECTIONS: Questions 14 through 18 are to be answered SOLELY on the basis of the
              information, the assumptions, and the table given below.

        Each question describes an applicant family. You are to determine into which of the four
categories (A, B, C, or D) each of the applicant families should be placed. In order to do this, you
must match the description of the applicant family with the factors determining eligibility for each of
the four categories. Each applicant family must meet ALL of the criteria for the category.

ASSUMPTIONS FOR ALL QUESTIONS
        The information in the following tables does NOT necessarily reflect actual practice in the
        Department of Social Services.
    1.   The date of application is January 25.
            Each applicant family that cannot be placed in categories A, B, or C must be placed in
    category D.
    2.   A *dependent child* is a child who is less than 18 years of age, or less than 21 years
    of age if attending school full time, who depends upon its parents for support.
    3.   A mother in a family with one or more dependent children is not expected to work and
    her work status is not to be considered in establishing the category of the family.

CATEGORY OF APPLICANT FAMILY	FACTORS DETERMINING ELIGIBILITY

A	1. There is at least one dependent child in the home.
	2. Children are deprived of parental support because father is:
	   (a) Deceased
	   (b) Absent from the home
	   (c) Incapacitated due to medically verified illness
	   (d) Over age 65
	   (e) Not fully employed because of verified ill health
	3. Parents or guardians reside in the same home as the children.
	4. Applicant family must have resided in the State for a period of one year or more.

B	1. There is at least one dependent child in the home. 2. Both parents are in the home and are not incapacitated. 3. Both parents are the children's natural parents. 4. Father unemployed or works less than 70 hours per month. 5. Father has recent work history. 6. Father not currently receiving Unemployment Insurance Benefits. 7. Father available and willing to work. 8. Applicant family must have resided in the State for a period of one year or more.
C	1. There is a war veteran in the home. 2. Applicant families do not meet the criteria for Categories A or B.
D	Applicant families do not meet the criteria for Categories A, B, or C

14. Woman, aged 52, with child 6 years old who she states was left in her home at the age of 2. Woman states child is her niece, and that she has no knowledge of whereabouts of parents or any other relatives. Both woman and child have resided in the State since June 15.

14. ____

15. Married couple with 2 dependent children at home. Family has resided in the State for the last 5 years. Wife cannot work. Husband, veteran of Gulf War, can work only 15 hours a week due to kidney ailment (verified).

15. ____

16. Married couple, both aged 35, with 3 dependent children at home, 1 of whom is 17 years of age. Wife available for work and presently working 2 days a week, 7 hours each day. Husband, who was laid off two weeks ago, is not eligible for Unemployment Insurance Benefits. Family has resided in the State since January 1, 2002.

16.____

17. Married couple with 1 dependent child at home. They have resided in the State since January 25, 2001. Wife must remain home to take care of child. Husband veteran of Gulf War. Husband is available for work on a limited basis because of heart condition which has been verified. A second child, a married 17-year-old son, lives in California.

17.____

18. Married couple with 2 children, ages 6 and 12, at home. Family has resided in the State since June 2, 1998. Wife not available for work. Husband, who served in the Iraqi War, was laid off 3 weeks ago and is receiving Unemployment Insurance Benefits of $500.00 weekly.

18.____

19. Of the following, the MOST important reason for referring a public assistance client for employment or training is to
    A. give him self-confidence
    B. make him self-supporting
    C. have him learn a new trade
    D. take him off the streets

19.____

20. Sometimes clients become silent during interviews.
    Of the following, the MOST probable reason for such silence is that the client is
    A. getting ready to tell a lie
    B. of low intelligence and does not know the answers to your questions
    C. thinking things over or has nothing more to say on the subject
    D. wishing he were not on welfare

20.____

KEY (CORRECT ANSWERS)

1. D	6. D	11. B	16. B
2. B	7. B	12. D	17. A
3. A	8. C	13. C	18. C
4. C	9. A	14. D	19. B
5. C	10. C	15. A	20. C

EXAMINATION SECTION
TEST 1

DIRECTIONS: Each question or incomplete statement is followed by several suggested answers or completions. Select the one that BEST answers the question or completes the statement. *PRINT THE LETTER OF THE CORRECT ANSWER IN THE SPACE AT THE RIGHT.*

Questions 1-4.

DIRECTIONS: Questions 1 through 4 are to be answered SOLELY on the basis of the information in the paragraphs below.

Some authorities have questioned whether the term "culture of poverty" should be used since "culture" means a design for living which is passed down from generation to generation. The culture of poverty is, however, a very useful concept if it is used with care, with recognition that poverty is a subculture, and with avoidance of the "cookie-cutter" approach. With regard to the individual, the cookie-cutter view assumes that all individuals in a culture turn out exactly alike, as if they were so many cookies. It overlooks the fact that, at least in our urban society, every individual is a member of more than one subculture; and which subculture most strongly influences his response in a given situation depends on the interaction of a great many factors, including his individual makeup and history, the specifics of the various subcultures to which he belongs, and the specifics of the given situation. It is always important to avoid the cookie-cutter view of culture, with regard to the individual and to the culture or subculture involved.

With regard to the culture as a whole, the cookie-cutter concept again assumes homogeneity and consistency. It forgets that within any one culture or subculture there are conflicts and contradictions, and that at any given moment an individual may have to choose, consciously, between conflicting values or patterns. Also, most individuals, in varying degrees, have a dual set of values - those by which they live and those they cherish as best. This point has been made and documented repeatedly about the culture of poverty.

1. The *cookie-cutter* approach assumes that
   A. members of the same *culture* are all alike
   B. *culture* stays the same from generation to generation
   C. the term *culture* should not be applied to groups who are poor
   D. there are value conflicts within most cultures

1.____

2. According to the passage, every person in our cities
   A. is involved in the conflicts of urban culture
   B. recognizes that poverty is a subculture
   C. lives by those values to which he is exposed
   D. belongs to more than one subculture

2.____

3. The above passage emphasizes that a culture is likely to contain within it
   A. one dominant set of values
   B. a number of contradictions

3.____

C. one subculture to which everyone belongs
D. members who are exactly alike

4. According to the above passage, individuals are sometimes forced to choose between   4._____

    A. cultures
    B. subcultures
    C. different sets of values
    D. a new culture and an old culture

Questions 5-8.

DIRECTIONS: Questions 5 through 8 are to be answered SOLELY on the basis of the following passage.

    There are approximately 33 million poor people in the United States; 14.3 million of them are children, 5.3 million are old people, and the remainder are in other categories. Altogether, 6.5 million families live in poverty because the heads of the households cannot works they are either too old or too sick or too severely handicapped, or they are widowed or deserted mothers of young children. There are the working poor, the low-paid workers, the workers in seasonal industries, and soldiers with no additional income who are heads of families. There are the underemployed: those who would like full-time jobs but cannot find them, those employees who would like year-round work but lack the opportunity, and those who are employed below their level of training. There are the non-working poor: the older men and women With small retirement incomes and those with no income, the disabled, the physically and mentally handicapped, and the chronically sick.

5. According to the above passage, APPROXIMATELY what percent of the poor people in   5._____
the United States are children?

    A. 33   B. 16   C. 20   D. 44

6. According to the above passage, people who work in seasonal industries are LIKELY to   6._____
be classified as

    A. working poor   B. underemployed
    C. non-working poor   D. low-paid workers

7. According to the above passage, the category of non-working poor includes people who   7._____

    A. receive unemployment insurance
    B. cannot find full-time work
    C. are disabled or mentally handicapped
    D. are soldiers with wives and children

8. According to the above passage, among the underemployed are those who   8._____

    A. can find only part-time work
    B. are looking for their first jobs
    C. are inadequately trained
    D. depend on insufficient retirement incomes

Questions 9-18.

DIRECTIONS: Questions 9 through 18 are to be answered SOLELY on the basis of the information given in the following charts.

CHILD CARE SERVICES 1997-2001

CHILDREN IN FOSTER HOMES AND VOLUNTARY INSTITUTIONS, BY TYPE OF CARE, IN NEW YORK CITY AND UPSTATE* NEW YORK

Year End	FOSTER FAMILY HOMES			Total in Foster Family Homes	Total in Voluntary Institutions	Total in Other	Total Number of Children
	Boarding Homes	Adoptive or Free Homes	Wage, Work or Self-Supportine				
New York City							
1997	12,389	1,773	33	14,195	7,187	1,128	22,510
1998	13,271	1,953	42	15,266	7,227	1,237	23,730
1999	14,012	2,134	32	16,178	7,087	1,372	24,637
2000	14,558	2,137	29	16,724	6,717	1,437	24,778
2001	14,759	2,241	37	17,037	6,777	1,455	25,264
Upstate							
1997	14,801	2,902	90	17,793	3,012	241	21,046
1998	15,227	2,943	175	18,345	3,067	291	21,703
1999	16,042	3,261	64	19,367	2,940	273	22,580
2000	16,166	3,445	60	19,671	2,986	362	23,121
2001	16,357	3,606	55	20,018	3.024	485	23,527

Upstate is defined as all of New York State, excluding New York City.

NUMBER OF CHILDREN, BY AGE, UNDER FOSTER FAMILY CARE IN NEW YORK CITY IN 2001

Borough	Children's Ages					Total All Ages
	One Year or Younger	Two Years	Three Years	Four Years	Over Four Years	
Manhattan	1,054	1,170	1,060	1,325	445	5,070
Bronx	842	1,196	1,156	1,220	484	4,882
Brooklyn	707	935	470	970	361	?
Queens	460	555	305	793	305	2,418
Richmond	270	505	160	173	112	1.224
Total All Boroughs	3,337	4,361	3,151	4,481	?	17,037

9.   According to the table, Child Care Services, 1997-2001, the number of children in New York City boarding homes was AT LEAST twice the number of children in New York City voluntary institutions in _____ of the five years.

9.____

   A. *only* one   B. *only* two   C. *only* three   D. all

10. If the number of children cared for in voluntary institutions in New York State increases from 2001 to 2002 by exactly the same number as from 2000 to 2001, then the 2002 year-end total of children in voluntary institutions in New York State will be

    A. 3,062   B. 6,837   C. 7,494   D. 9,899

10.____

11. If the total number of children under child care services in New York City in 1997 was 25% more than in 1996, then the 1996 New York City total was MOST NEARLY

    A. 11,356   B. 11,647   C. 16,883   D. 18,008

11.____

12. From 1997 through 2001, the New York State five-year average of children in Child Care Services classified as *other* is MOST NEARLY

    A. 330   B. 728   C. 1,326   D. 1,656

12.____

13. Of all the children under foster family care in the Bronx in 2001, the percentage who were one year of age or younger is MOST NEARLY

    A. 16%   B. 17%   C. 18%   D. 19%

13.____

14. Suppose that in New York State the *wage, work, or self-supporting* type of foster family care is given only to children between the ages of 14 and 18, and that, of the children in *adoptive or free home* foster care in each of the five years listed, only one percent each year are between the ages of 14 and 18.
The TOTAL number of 14 to 18-year-olds under foster family care in Upstate New York exceeded 95 in _____ of the five years.

    A. each   B. four   C. three   D. two

14.____

15. The average number of two-year-olds under foster family care in New York City's boroughs in 2001 is MOST NEARLY

    A. 872   B. 874   C. 875   D. 882

15.____

16. The difference between the total number of children of all ages under foster family care in Brooklyn in 2001 and the total number under foster care in Richmond that year is

    A. 1,224   B. 2,219   C. 3,443   D. 4,667

16.____

17. Suppose that by the end of 2002 the number of children one year or younger under foster family care in Queens will be twice the 2001 total, while the number of two-year-olds will be four-fifths the 2001 total.
The 2002 total of children two years or younger under foster family care in Queens will be

    A. 2,418   B. 1,624   C. 1,364   D. 1,015

17.____

18. The TOTAL number oi children over four years of age under foster care in New York City in 2001 was

    A. 1,607   B. 1,697   C. 1,707   D. 1,797

18.____

19. At the start of a year, a family was receiving a public assistance grant of $191 twice a month, on the 1st and 15th of each month. On March 1, their rent allowance was decreased from $75 to $71 a month since they had moved to a smaller apartment. On August 1, their semimonthly food allowance, which had been $40.20, was raised by 10%. In that year, the TOTAL amount of money disbursed to this family was

    A. $2,272.10   B. $3,290.70
    C. $4,544.20   D. $4,584.20

19._____

20. It is discovered that a client has received double public assistance for 2 months by having been enrolled at two service centers of the Department of Social Services. The client should have received $84.00 twice a month instead of the double amount. He now agrees to repay the money by equal deductions from his public assistance check over a period of 12 months.
What will the amount of his NEXT check be?

    A. $56   B. $70   C. $77   D. $80

20._____

21. Suppose a study is being made of the composition of 3,550 families receiving public assistance. Of the first 1,050 families reviewed, 18% had four or more children.
If, in the remaining number of families, the percentage with four or more children is half as high as the percentage in the group already reviewed, then the percentage of families with four or more children in the entire group of families is MOST NEARLY

    A. 12   B. 14   C. 16   D. 27

21._____

22. Suppose that food prices have risen 13%, and an increase of the same amount has been granted in the food allotment given to people receiving public assistance.
If a family has been receiving $405 a month, 35% of which is allotted for food, then the TOTAL amount of public assistance this family receives per month will be changed to

    A. $402.71   B. $420.03   C. $423.43   D. $449.71

22._____

23. Assume that the food allowance is to be raised 5% in August but will be retroactive for four months to April. The retroactive allowance is to be divided into equal sections and added to the public assistance checks for August, September, October, November, and December.
A family which has been receiving $420 monthly, 40% of which was allotted for food, will receive what size check in August?

    A. $426.72   B. $428.40   C. $430.50   D. $435.12

23._____

24. A blind client, who receives $105 public assistance twice a month, inherits 14 shares of stock worth $90 each. The client is required to sell the stock and spend his inheritance before receiving more public assistance.
Using his public assistance allowance as a guide, how many months are his new assets expected to last?

    A. 6   B. 7   C. 8   D. 12

24._____

25. The Department of Social Services has 16 service centers in Manhattan. These centers   25.____
may be divided into those which are downtown (south of Central Park) and those which
are uptown. Two of the centers are special service centers and are downtown, while the
remainder of the centers are general service centers. There is a total of 7 service centers
downtown.
The percentage of the general service centers which are uptown is MOST NEARLY

   A. 56   B. 64   C. 69   D. 79

KEY (CORRECT ANSWERS)

1. A	11. D
2. D	12. D
3. B	13. B
4. C	14. C
5. D	15. A
6. A	16. B
7. C	17. C
8. A	18. C
9. B	19. D
10. D	20. B

21. A
22. C
23. D
24. A
25. B

TEST 2

DIRECTIONS: Each question or incomplete statement is followed by several suggested answers or completions. Select the one that BEST answers the question or completes the statement. *PRINT THE LETTER OF THE CORRECT ANSWER IN THE SPACE AT THE RIGHT.*

1. On January 1, a family was receiving supplementary monthly public assistance of $56 for food, $48 for rent, and $28 for other necessities. In the spring, their rent rose by 10%, and their rent allowance was adjusted accordingly.
   In the summer, due to the death of a family member, their allotments for food and other necessities were reduced by 1/7.
   Their monthly allowance check in the fall should be   1.____

   A. $124.80   B. $128.80   C. $132.80   D. $136.80

2. Twice a month, a certain family receives a $170 general allowance for rent, food, and clothing expenses. In addition, the family receives a specific supplementary allotment for utilities of $192 a year, which is added to their semi-monthly check.
   If the general allowance alone is reduced by 5%, what will be the TOTAL amount of their next semi-monthly check?   2.____

   A. $161.50   B. $169.50   C. $170.00   D. $177.50

3. If each clerk in a certain unit sees an average of 9 clients in a 7-hour day and there are 15 clerks in the unit, APPROXIMATELY how many clients will be seen in a 35-hour week?   3.____

   A. 315   B. 405   C. 675   D. 945

4. The program providing federal welfare aid to the state and its cities is intended to expand services to public assistance recipients.
   All of the following services are included in the program EXCEPT   4.____

   A. homemaker/housekeeper services
   B. mental health clinics
   C. abortion clinics
   D. narcotic addiction control services

5. The Department of Consumer Affairs is NOT concerned with regulation of   5.____

   A. prices   B. product service guarantees
   C. welfare fraud   D. product misrepresentation

6. A plan to control the loss of welfare monies would likely contain all of the following EXCEPT   6.____

   A. identification cards with photographs of the welfare client
   B. individual cash payments to each member of a family
   C. computerized processing of welfare money records
   D. face-to-face interviews with the welfare clients

7. The state law currently allows a woman to obtain an abortion   7._____

    A. only if it is intended to save her life
    B. if three doctors confirm the need for such treatment
    C. if it does not conflict with her religious beliefs
    D. upon her request, up to the 24th week of pregnancy

8. Under the city's public assistance program, allocations for payment of a client's rent and   8._____
    security deposits are given in check form directly to the welfare recipient and not to the
    landlord.
    This practice is used in the city MAINLY as an effort to

    A. increase the client's responsibility for his own affairs
    B. curb the rent overcharges made by most landlords in the city
    C. control the number of welfare recipients housed in public housing projects
    D. limit the number of checks issued to each welfare family

9. The city plans to save 100 million dollars a year in public assistance costs.   9._____
    To achieve this goal, the Human Resources Administration and the Department of
    Social Services may take any of the following steps EXCEPT

    A. tightening controls on public assistance eligibility requirements
    B. intensifying the investigations of relief frauds
    C. freezing the salaries of all agency employees for a one-year period
    D. cutting the services extended to public assistance clients

10. Recently, the state instituted a work relief program under which employable recipients of   10._____
    Home Relief and Aid to Dependent Children are given jobs to help work off their relief
    grants.
    Under the present work relief program, program recipients are NOT required to

    A. report to state employment offices every two weeks to pick up their welfare checks
    B. live within a two-mile radius of the job site to which they are referred
    C. respond to offers of part-time jobs in public agencies
    D. take job training courses offered through the State Employment Service

11. Of the following, the MOST inclusive program designed to help selected cities to sub-   11._____
    stantially improve social, physical, and economic conditions in specially selected slum
    neighborhoods is known as the

    A. Model Cities Program
    B. Neighborhood Youth Corps Program
    C. Urban Renewal Program
    D. Emergency Employment Act

12. The crusade against environmental hazards in the United States is concentrated in   12._____
    urban areas MOSTLY on the problems of

    A. air pollution, sewage treatment, and noise
    B. garbage collection
    C. automobile exhaust fumes and street cleanliness
    D. recycling, reconstitution, and open space

Questions 13-16.

DIRECTIONS: Questions 13 through 16 are to be answered SOLELY on the basis of the information in the following passage.

*City social work agencies and the police have been meeting at City Hall to coordinate
efforts to defuse the tensions among teenage groups that they fear could flare into warfare
once summer vacations begin. Police intelligence units, with the help of the District Attorneys'
offices, are gathering information to identify gangs and their territories. A list of 3, 000 gang
members has already been assembled, and 110 gangs have been identified. Social workers
from various agencies like the Department of Social Services, Neighborhood youth Corps,
and the Youth Board are out every day developing liaison with groups of juveniles through
meetings at schools and recreation centers. Many street workers spend their days seeking to
ease the intergang hostility, tracing potentially incendiary rumors, and trying to channel willing
gang members into participation in established summer programs. The city's Youth Services
Agency plans to spend a million dollars for special summer programs in ten main city areas
where gang activity is most firmly entrenched. Five of the "gang neighborhoods" are clustered
in an area forming most of southeastern Bronx, and it is here that most of the 110 identified
gangs have formed. Special Youth Services programs will also be directed toward the Rock-
away section of Queens, Chinatown, Washington Heights, and two neighborhoods in north-
ern Staten Island noted for a lot of motorcycle gang activity. Some of these programs will
emphasize sports and recreation, others vocational guidance or neighborhood improvement,
but each program will be aimed at benefiting all youngsters in the area. Although none of the
money will be spent specifically on gang members, the Youth Services Agency is consulting
gang leaders, along with other teenagers, on the projects they would like developed in their
area.*

13.   The above passage states that one of the steps taken by street workers in trying to   13.____
defuse the tensions among teenage gangs is that of

      A.   conducting summer school sessions that will benefit all neighborhood youth
      B.   monitoring neighborhood sports competitions between rival gangs
      C.   developing liaison with community school boards and parent associations
      D.   tracing rumors that could intensify intergang hostilities

14.   Based on the information given in the above passage on gangs and New York City's   14.____
gang members, it is CORRECT to state that

      A.   there are no teenage gangs located in Brooklyn
      B.   most of the gangs identified by the police are concentrated in one borough
      C.   there is a total of 110 gangs in New York City
      D.   only a small percentage of gangs in New York City is in Queens

15.   According to the above passage, one IMPORTANT aspect of the program is that   15.____

      A.   youth gang leaders and other teenagers are involved in the planning
      B.   money will be given directly to gang members for use on their projects
      C.   only gang members will be allowed to participate in the programs
      D.   the parents of gang members will act as youth leaders

16. Various city agencies are cooperating in the attempt to keep the city's youth *cool* during the summer school vacation period.

The above passage does NOT specifically indicate participation in this project by the

    A. Police Department
    B. District Attorney's Office
    C. Board of Education
    D. Department of Social Services

16._____

Questions 17-19.

DIRECTIONS: Questions 17 through 19 are to be answered SOLELY on the basis of the infor- mation in the following passage.

It is important that interviewers understand to some degree the manner in which stereo- typed thinking operates. Stereotypes are commonly held, but predominantly false, precon- ceptions about the appearance and traits of individuals of different racial, religious, ethnic, and subcultural groups. Distinct traits, physical and mental, are associated with each group, and membership in a particular group is enough, in the mind of a person holding the stereo- type, to assure that these traits will be perceived in individuals who are members of that group. Conversely, possession of the particular stereotyped trait by an individual usually indi- cates to the holder of the stereotype that the individual is a group member. Linked to the for- mation of stereotypes is the fact that mental traits, either positive or negative, such as honesty, laziness, avariciousness, and other characteristics are associated with particular stereotypes. Either kind of stereotype, if held by an interviewer, can seriously damage the results of an interview. In general, stereotypes can be particularly dangerous when they are part of the belief patterns of administrators, interviewers, and supervisors, who are in a posi- tion to affect the lives of others and to stimulate or retard the development of human potential. The holding of a stereotype by an interviewer, for example, diverts his attention from signifi- cant essential facts and information upon which really valid assessments may be made. Unfortunately, it is the rare interviewer who is completely conscious of the real basis upon which he is making his evaluation of the people he is interviewing. The specific reasons given by an interviewer for a negative evaluation, even though apparently logical and based upon what, in the mind of the interviewer, are very good reasons, may not be the truly motivating factors. This is why the careful selection and training of interviewers is such an important responsibility of an agency which is attempting to help a great diversity of human beings.

17. Of the following, the BEST title for the above paragraph is

    A. POSITIVE AND NEGATIVE EFFECTS OF STEREOTYPED THINKING
    B. THE RELATIONSHIP OF STEREOTYPES TO INTERVIEWING
    C. AN AGENCY'S RESPONSIBILITY IN INTERVIEWING
    D. THE IMPACT OF STEREOTYPED THINKING ON PROFESSIONAL FUNCTIONS

17._____

18. According to the above passage, MOST interviewers

    A. compensate for stereotyped beliefs to avoid negatively affecting the results of their interviews
    B. are influenced by stereotypes they hold, but put greater stress on factual informa- tion developed during the interview
    C. are seldom aware of their real motives when evaluating interviewees
    D. give logical and good reasons for negative evaluations of interviewees

18._____

19. According to the above passage, which of the following is NOT a characteristic of stereotypes?

    A. Stereotypes influence estimates of personality traits of people.
    B. Positive stereotypes can damage the results of an interview.
    C. Physical traits associated with stereotypes seldom really exist.
    D. Stereotypes sometimes are a basis upon which valid personality assessments can
       be made.

19._____

Questions 20-25.

DIRECTIONS: Questions 20 through 25 are to be answered SOLELY on the basis of the information in the following passage.

*The quality of the voice of a worker is an important factor in conveying to clients and co-
workers his attitude and, to some degree, his character. The human voice, when not consciously disguised, may reflect a person's mood, temper, and personality. It has been shown
in several experiments that certain character traits can be assessed with better than chance
accuracy through listening to the voice of an unknown person who cannot be seen.*

*Since one of the objectives of the worker is to put clients at ease and to present an
encouraging and comfortable atmosphere, a harsh, shrill, or loud voice could have a negative
effect. A client who displays emotions of anger or resentment would probably be provoked
even further by a caustic tone. In a face-to-face situation, an unpleasant voice may be com-
pensated for to some degree by a concerned and kind facial expression. However, when one
speaks on the telephone, the expression on one's face cannot be seen by the listener. A
supervising clerk who wishes to represent himself effectively to clients should try to eliminate
as many faults as possible in striving to develop desirable voice qualities.*

20. If a worker uses a sarcastic tone while interviewing a resentful client, the client, according to the above passage, would MOST likely

    A. avoid the face-to-face situation
    B. be ashamed of his behavior
    C. become more resentful
    D. be provoked to violence

20._____

21. According to the above passage, experiments comparing voice and character traits have
demonstrated that

    A. prospects for improving an unpleasant voice through training are better than
       chance
    B. the voice can be altered to project many different psychological characteristics
    C. the quality of the human voice reveals more about the speaker than his words do
    D. the speaker's voice tells the hearer something about the speaker's personality

21._____

22. Which of the following, according to the above passage, is a person's voice MOST likely
to reveal?
His

    A. prejudices
    C. social awareness
                           B. intelligence
                           D. temperament

22._____

23. It may be MOST reasonably concluded from the above passage that an interested and sympathetic expression on the face of a worker

    23.____

    A.   may induce a client to feel certain he will receive welfare benefits
    B.   will eliminate the need for pleasant vocal qualities in the interviewer
    C.   may help to make up for an unpleasant voice in the interviewer
    D.   is desirable as the interviewer speaks on the telephone to a client

24. Of the following, the MOST reasonable implication of the above paragraph is that a worker should, when speaking to a client, control and use his voice to

    24.____

    A.   simulate a feeling of interest in the problems of the client
    B.   express his emotions directly and adequately
    C.   help produce in the client a sense of comfort and security
    D.   reflect his own true personality

25. It may be concluded from the passage that the PARTICULAR reason for a worker to pay special attention to modulating her voice when talking on the phone to a client is that, during a telephone conversation,

    25.____

    A.   there is a necessity to compensate for the way in which a telephone distorts the voice
    B.   the voice of the worker is a reflection of her mood and character
    C.   the client can react only on the basis of the voice and words she hears
    D.   the client may have difficulty getting a clear understanding over the telephone

---

KEY (CORRECT ANSWERS)

1.	A		11.	A
2.	B		12.	A
3.	C		13.	D
4.	C		14.	B
5.	C		15.	A
6.	B		16.	C
7.	D		17.	B
8.	A		18.	C
9.	C		19.	D
10.	B		20.	C

21.	D
22.	D
23.	C
24.	C
25.	C

EXAMINATION SECTION
TEST 1

DIRECTIONS: Each question or incomplete statement is followed by several suggested answers or completions. Select the one that BEST answers the question or completes the statement. *PRINT THE LETTER OF THE CORRECT ANSWER IN THE SPACE AT THE RIGHT.*

1. You find that an applicant for public assistance is hesitant about showing you some required personal material and documents. Your INITIAL reaction to this situation should be to

   A. quietly insist that he give you the required materials
   B. make an exception in his case to avoid making him uncomfortable
   C. suspect that he may be trying to withhold evidence
   D. understand that he is in a stressful situation and may feel ashamed to reveal such information

1.____

2. An applicant has just given you a response which does not seem clear. Of the following. the BEST course of action for you to take in order to check your understanding of the applicant's response is for you to

   A. ask the question again during a subsequent interview with this applicant
   B. repeat the applicant's answer in the applicant.s own words and ask if that is what the applicant meant
   C. later in the interview, repeat the question that led to this response
   D. repeat the question that led to this response, but say it more forcefully

2.____

3. While speaking with applicants for public assistance, you may find that there are times when an applicant will be silent for a short while before answering questions. In order to gather the BEST information from the applicant, the interviewer should *generally* treat these silences by

   A. repeating the same question to make the applicant stop hesitating
   B. rephrasing the question in a way that the applicant can answer it faster
   C. directing an easier question to the applicant so that he can gain confidence in answering
   D. waiting patiently and not pressuring the applicant into quick undeveloped answers

3.____

4. In dealing with members of different ethnic and religious groups among the applicants you interview, you should give

   A. individuals the services to which they are entitled
   B. less service to those you judge to be more advantaged
   C. better service to groups with which you sympathize most
   D. better service to group with political *muscle*

4.____

5. You must be sure that, when interviewing an applicant, you phrase each question carefully. Of the following, the MOST important reason for this is to insure that

   A. the applicant will phrase each of his responses carefully
   B. you use correct grammar
   C. it is clear to the applicant what information you are seeking
   D. you do not word the same question differently for different applicants

5.____

6. When given a form to complete, a client hesitates, tells you that he cannot fill out forms too well, and that he is afraid he will do a poor job. He asks you to do it for him. You are quite sure, however, that he is able to do it himself. In this case, it would be MOST advisable for you to

    A. encourage him to try filling out the application as well as he can
    B. fill out the application for him
    C. explain to him that he must learn to accept responsibility
    D. tell him that, if others can fill out an application, he can too

6.____

7. Assume that an applicant for public assistance whom you are interviewing has made a statement that is obviously not true. Of the following, the BEST course of action for you to take at this point in the interview is to

    A. ask the applicant if he is sure about his statement
    B. tell the applicant that his statement is incorrect
    C. question the applicant further to clarify his response
    D. assume that the statement is true

7.____

8. Assume that you are conducting an initial interview with an applicant for public assistance. Of the following, the MOST advisable questions for you to ask at the beginning of this interview are questions that

    A. can be answered in one or two sentences
    B. have nothing to do with the subject matter of the interview
    C. are most likely to reveal any hostility on the part of the applicant
    D. the applicant is most likely to be willing and able to answer

8.____

9. When interviewing a particularly nervous and upset applicant for public assistance, the one of the following actions which you should take FIRST is to

    A. inform the applicant that, to be helped, he must cooperate
    B. advise the applicant that proof must be provided for statements he makes
    C. assure the applicant that every effort will be made to provide him with whatever assistance he is entitled to
    D. tell the applicant he will have no trouble obtaining public assistance so long as he is truthful

9.____

10. Assume that, following normal routine, it is part of your job to prepare a monthly report for your unit head that eventually goes to the Director of your Center. The report contains information on the number of applicants you have interviewed that have been approved for different types of public assistance and the number of applicants you have interviewed that have been turned down. Errors on such reports are *serious* because

    A. you are expected to be able to prove how many applicants you have interviewed each month
    B. accurate statistics are needed for effective management of the department
    C. they may not be discovered before the report is transmitted to the Center Director
    D. they may result in a loss of assistance to the applicants left out of the report

10.____

11. During interviews, people give information about themselves in several ways. Which of   11.____
the following *usually* gives the LEAST amount of information about the person being
questioned? His

    A. spoken words   B. tone of voice
    C. facial expression   D. body position

12. Suppose an applicant, while being interviewed about his eligibility for public assistance,   12.____
becomes angered by your questioning and begins to use sharp, uncontrolled language.
Which of the following is the BEST way for you to react to him?

    A. Speak in his style to show him that you are neither impressed nor upset by his
        speech
    B. Interrupt him and tell him that you are not required to listen to this kind of speech
    C. Lower your voice and slow the rate of your speech in an attempt to set an example
        that will calm him
    D. Let him continue in his way but insist that he answer your questions directly

13. You have been informed that no determination has yet been made on the eligibility of an   13.____
applicant for public assistance. The decision depends on further checking. His situation,
however, is similar to that of many other applicants whose eligibility has been approved.
The applicant calls you, quite worried, and asks you whether his application has been
accepted. What would be BEST for you to do under these circumstances? Tell him

    A. his application is being checked and you will let him know the final result as soon
        as possible
    B. that a written request addressed to your supervisor will probably get faster action
        for his case
    C. not to worry since other applicants with similar backgrounds have already been
        accepted
    D. since there is no definite information and you are very busy, you will call him back

14. Suppose that you have been talking with an applicant for public assistance. You have the   14.____
feeling from the latest things the applicant has said that some of his answers to earlier
questions were not totally correct. You guess that he might have been afraid or confused
earlier but that your conversation has now put him in a more comfortable frame of mind.
In order to test the reliability of information received from the earlier questions, the BEST
thing for you to do *now* is to ask new questions that

    A. allow the applicant to explain why he deliberately gave false information to you
    B. ask for the same information, although worded differently from the original ques-
        tions
    C. put pressure on the applicant so that he personally wants to clear up the facts in
        his earlier answers
    D. indicate to the applicant that you are aware of his decept iveness

15. Assume that you are a supervisor. While providing you with required information, an   15.____
applicant for public assistance informs you that she does not know who is the father of
her child. Of the following, the MOST advisable action for you to take is to

    A. ask her to explain further
    B. advise her about birth control facilities
    C. express your sympathy for the situation
    D. go on to the next item of information

16. If, in an interview, you wish to determine a client.s usual occupation, which one of the fol-   16.____
lowing questions is MOST likely to elicit the most useful information?

    A. Did you ever work in a factory?
    B. Do you know how to do office work?
    C. What kind of work do you do?
    D. Where are you working now?

17. Assume that, in the course of the day, you are approached by a clerk from another office   17.____
who starts questioning you about one of the clients you have just interviewed. The clerk
says that she is a relative of the client. According to departmental policy, all matters discussed with clients are to be kept confidential. Of the following, the BEST course of
action for you to take in this situation would be to

    A. check to see whether the clerk is really a relative before you make any further deci-
       sion
    B. explain to the clerk why you cannot divulge the information
    C. tell the clerk that you do not know the answers to her questions
    D. tell the clerk that she can get from the client any information the client wishes to
       give

18. Which of the following is *usually* the BEST technique for you, as an interviewer, to use to   18.____
bring an applicant back to subject matter from which the applicant has strayed?

    A. Ask the applicant a question that is related to the subject of the interview
    B. Show the applicant that his response is unrelated to the question
    C. Discreetly remind the applicant that there is a time allotment for the interview
    D. Tell the applicant that you will be happy to discuss the extraneous matters at a
       future interview

19. Assume that you notice that one of the clerks has accidentally pulled the wrong form to   19.____
give to her client. Of the following, the BEST way for you to handle this situation would be
to tell

    A. the clerk about her error, and precisely describe the problems that will result
    B. the clerk about her error in an understanding and friendly way
    C. the clerk about her error in a humorous way and tell her that no real damage was
       done
    D. your supervisor that clerks need more training in the use and application of depart-
       mental forms

20. Of the following characteristics, the one which would be MOST valuable when helping an   20.____
angry applicant to understand why he has received less assistance than he believes he
is entitled to would be the ability to

    A. state the rules exactly as they apply to the applicant's problem
    B. cite examples of other cases where the results have been similar
    C. remain patient and understanding of the person's feelings
    D. remain completely objective and uninvolved in individual personal problems

21. Reports are usually divided into several sections, some of which are more necessary   21.____
    than others. Of the following, the section which is MOST often necessary to include in a
    report is a(n)

    A. table of contents   B. introduction
    C. index   D. bibliography

22. Suppose you are writing a report on an interview you have just completed with a particu-   22.____
    larly hostile applicant for public assistance. Which of the following BEST describes what
    you should include in this report?

    A. What you think caused the applicant.s hostile attitude during the interview
    B. Specific examples of the applicant.s hostile remarks and behavior
    C. The relevant information uncovered during the interview
    D. A recommendation that the applicant.s request be denied because of his hostility

23. When including recommendations in a report to your supervisor, which of the following is   23.____
    MOST important for you to do?

    A. Provide several alternative courses of action for each recommendation
    B. First present the supporting evidence, then the recommendations
    C. First present the recommendations, then the supporting evidence
    D. Make sure the recommendations arise logically out of the information in the report

24. It is often necessary that the writer of a report present facts and sufficient arguments to   24.____
    gain acceptance of the points, conclusions, or recommendations set forth in the report.
    Of the following, the LEAST advisable step to take in organizing a report, when such
    argumentation is the important factor, is a(n)

    A. elaborate expression of personal belief
    B. businesslike discussion of the problem as a whole
    C. orderly arrangement of convincing data
    D. reasonable explanation of the primary issues

25. Suppose you receive a phone call from an applicant about a problem which requires that   25.____
    you must look up the information and call her back. Although the applicant had given you
    her name earlier and you can pronounce the name, you are not sure that you can spell it
    correctly. Asking the applicant to spell her name is

    A. *good,* because this indicates to the applicant that you intend to obtain the informa-
       tion she requested
    B. *poor,* because she may feel you are making fun of her name
    C. *good,* because you will be sure to get the correct name
    D. *poor,* because she will think you have not been listening to her

KEY (CORRECT ANSWERS)

1.	D		11.	D
2.	B		12.	C
3.	D		13.	A
4.	A		14.	B
5.	C		15.	D
6.	A		16.	C
7.	C		17.	B
8.	D		18.	A
9.	C		19.	B
10.	B		20.	C

21.	B
22.	C
23.	D
24.	A
25.	C

———

TEST 2

DIRECTIONS: Each question or incomplete statement is followed by several suggested answers or completions. Select the one that BEST answers the question or completes the statement. *PRINT THE LETTER OF THE CORRECT ANSWER IN THE SPACE AT THE RIGHT.*

Questions 1-9.

DIRECTIONS: Answer Questions 1 through 9 SOLELY on the basis of the information in the following passage.

The establishment of a procedure whereby the client's rent is paid directly by the Social Service agency has been suggested recently by many people in the Social Service field. It is believed that such a procedure would be advantageous to both the agency and the client. Under the current system, clients often complain that their rent allowances are not for the correct amount. Agencies, in turn, have had to cope with irate landlords who complain that they are not receiving rent checks until much later than their due date.

The proposed new system would involve direct payment of the client's rent by the agency to the landlord. Clients would not receive a monthly rent allowance. Under one possible implementation of such a system, special rent payment offices would be set up in each borough and staffed by Social Service clerical personnel. Each office would handle all work involved in sending out monthly rent payments. Each client would receive monthly notification from the Social Service agency that his rent has been paid. A rent office would be established for every three Social Service centers in each borough. Only in cases where the rental exceeds $700 per month would payment be made and records kept by the Social Service center itself rather than a special rent office. However, clients would continue to make all direct contacts through the Social Service center.

Files in the rent offices would be organized on the basis of client rental. All cases involving monthly rents up to, but not exceeding, $300 would be placed in salmon-colored folders. Cases with rents from $301 to $500 would be placed in buff folders, and those with rents exceeding $500, but less than $700 would be filed in blue folders. If a client's rental changed, he would be required to notify the center as soon as possible so that this information could be brought up-to-date in his folder, and the color of his folder changed if necessary. Included in the information needed, in addition to the amount of rent, are the size of the apartment, the type of heat, and the number of flights of stairs to climb if there is no elevator.

Discussion as to whether the same information should be required of clients residing in city projects was resolved with the decision that the identical system of filing and updating of files should apply to such project tenants. The basic problem that might arise from the institution of such a program is that clients would resent being unable to pay their own rent. However, it is likely that such resentment would be only a temporary reaction to change and would disappear after the new system became standard procedure. It has been suggested that this program first be experimented with on a small scale to determine what problems may arise and how the program can be best implemented.

1. According to the passage, there are a number of complaints about the current system of rent payments. Which of the following is a *complaint* expressed in the passage?   1.____

    A. Landlords complain that clients sometimes pay the wrong amount for their rent.

    B. Landlords complain that clients sometimes do not pay their rent on time.

    C.   Clients say that the Social Service agency sometimes does not mail the rent out on time.

    D.   Landlords say that they sometimes fail to receive a check for the rent.

2.   Assume that there are 15 Social Service centers in Manhattan. According to the passage, the number of rent offices that should be established in that borough under the new system is   2._____

    A.   1   B.   3   C.   5   D.   15

3.   According to the passage, a client under the new system would receive   3._____

    A.   a rent receipt from the landlord indicating that Social Services has paid the rent
    B.   nothing since his rent has been paid by Social Services
    C.   verification from the landlord that the rent was paid
    D.   notices of rent payment from the Social Service agency

4.   According to the passage, a case record involving a client whose rent has changed from $310 to $540 per month should be changed from a _____ folder to a _____ folder.   4._____

    A.   blue; salmon-colored   B.   buff; blue
    C.   salmon-colored; blue   D.   yellow; buff

5.   According to the above passage, if a client's rental is lowered because of violations in his building, he would be required to notify the   5._____

    A.   building department   B.   landlord
    C.   rent payment office   D.   Social Service center

6.   Which one of the following kinds of information about a rented apartment is NOT mentioned in the above passage as being necessary to include in the client's folder? The   6._____

    A.   floor number, if in an apartment house with an elevator
    B.   rental, if in a city project apartment
    C.   size of the apartment, if in a two-family house
    D.   type of heat, if in a city project apartment

7.   Assume that the rent payment proposal discussed in the passage is approved and ready for implementation in the city. Which of the following actions is MOST in accordance with the proposal described in the above passage?   7._____

    A.   Change over completely and quickly to the new system to avoid the confusion of having clients under both systems.
    B.   Establish rent payment offices in all of the existing Social Service centers.
    C.   Establish one small rent payment office in Manhattan for about six months.
    D.   Set up an office in each borough and discontinue issuing rent allowances.

8.   According to the passage, it can be *inferred* that the MOST important drawback of the new system would be that once a program is started, clients might feel   8._____

    A.   they have less independence than they had before
    B.   unable to cope with problems that mature people should be able to handle
    C.   too far removed from Social Service personnel to successfully adapt to the new requirements
    D.   too independent to work with the system

9. The above passage suggests that the proposed rent program be started as a pilot program rather than be instituted immediately throughout the city. Of the following possible reasons for a pilot program, the one which is stated in the passage as the MOST direct reason is that

    A. any change made would then be only on a temporary basis
    B. difficulties should be determined from small-scale implementation
    C. implementation on a wide scale is extremely difficult
    D. many clients might resent the new system

9.____

10. A report is often revised several times before final preparation and distribution in an effort to make certain the report meets the needs of the situation for which it is designed.
Which of the following is the BEST way for the author to be sure that a report covers the areas he intended?

    A. Obtain a co-worker's opinion.
    B. Compare it with a content checklist.
    C. Test it on a subordinate.
    D. Check his bibliography.

10.____

11. Visual aids used in a report may be placed either in the text material or in the appendix. Deciding where to put a chart, table, or any such aid should depend on the

    A. title of the report   B. purpose of the visual aid
    C. title of the visual aid   D. length of the report

11.____

12. In which of the following situations is an oral report PREFERABLE to a written report? When a(n)

    A. recommendation is being made for a future plan of action
    B. department head requests immediate information
    C. long standing policy change is made
    D. analysis of complicated statistical data is involved

12.____

13. When an applicant is approved for public assistance, standard forms with certain information must be filled in.
The GREATEST advantage of using standard forms in this situation rather than writing the report as you see fit is that

    A. the report can be acted on quickly
    B. the report can be written without directions from a supervisor
    C. needed information is less likely to be left out of the report
    D. information that is written up this way is more likely to be verified

13.____

14. In some types of reports, visual aids add interest, meaning, and support. They also provide an essential means of effectively communicating the message of the report.
Of the following, the selection of the suitable visual aids to use with a report is LEAST dependent on the

    A. nature and scope of the report   B. way in which the aid is to be used
    C. aids used in other reports   D. prospective readers of the report

14.____

15. He wanted to ASCERTAIN the facts before arriving at a conclusion. The word ASCER-   15._____
    TAIN means *most nearly*

    A. disprove   B. determine   C. convert   D. provide

16. Did the supervisor ASSENT to her request for annual leave? The word ASSENT means   16._____
    most nearly

    A. allude   B. protest   C. agree   D. refer

17. The new worker was fearful that the others would REBUFF her. The word REBUFF   17._____
    means *most nearly*

    A. ignore   B. forget   C. copy   D. snub

18. The supervisor of that office does not CONDONE lateness. The word CONDONE means   18._____
    most nearly

    A. mind   B. excuse   C. punish   D. remember

19. Each employee was instructed to be as CONCISE as possible when preparing a report.   19._____
    The word CONCISE means *most nearly*

    A. exact   B. sincere   C. flexible   D. brief

20. Despite many requests for them, there was a SCANT supply of new blotters. The word   20._____
    SCANT means *most nearly*

    A. adequate   B. abundant
    C. insufficient   D. expensive

21. Did they REPLENISH the supply of forms in the cabinet? The word REPLENISH means   21._____
    most nearly

    A. straighten up   B. refill
    C. sort out   D. use

22. Employees may become bored if they are assigned DIVERSE duties. The word   22._____
    DIVERSE means *most nearly*

    A. interesting   B. different
    C. challenging   D. enjoyable

23. During the probation period, the worker proved to be INEPT. The word INEPT means   23._____
    most nearly

    A. incompetent   B. insubordinate
    C. satisfactory   D. uncooperative

24. The PUTATIVE father was not living with the family. The word PUTATIVE means *most*   24._____
    nearly

    A. reputed   B. unemployed
    C. concerned   D. indifferent

25. The adopted child researched various documents of VITAL STATISTICS in an effort to   25._____
    discover the names of his natural parents. The words VITAL STATISTICS means *most*
    nearly statistics relating to

    A. human life   B. hospitals
    C. important facts   D. health and welfare

KEY (CORRECT ANSWERS)

1.	B		11.	B
2.	C		12.	B
3.	D		13.	C
4.	B		14.	C
5.	D		15.	B
6.	A		16.	C
7.	C		17.	D
8.	A		18.	B
9.	B		19.	D
10.	B		20.	C

21.	B
22.	B
23.	A
24.	A
25.	A

———

EXAMINATION SECTION
TEST 1

DIRECTIONS: Each question or incomplete statement is followed by several suggested answers or completions. Select the one that BEST answers the question or completes the statement. *PRINT THE LETTER OF THE CORRECT ANSWER IN THE SPACE AT THE RIGHT.*

1. The purpose of an ethnic survey of city employees is to determine   1.____

    A.   the degree of *ethnic group identity* among city employees belonging to various minority groups
    B.   whether there has been job discrimination by city agencies against minority groups
    C.   the basis for the establishment of quotas which would guarantee jobs to a certain number of minority group members
    D.   a method of strengthening the merit system through establishment of discretionary hiring practices for minority group members

2. Of the following, an important purpose of the separation of the functions of income main-   2.____
    tenance and social services in the Department of Social Services is to

    A.   give caseworkers more time to provide services and counseling to welfare families and individuals
    B.   eliminate investigation of all families and individuals applying for public assistance
    C.   enable the Department of Social Services to implement the state-mandated program of check pickup at the State Employment Service
    D.   facilitate decentralization of the allocation of funds for services

3. Changes in the Food Stamp Program resulted in   3.____

    A.   *raising* both the maximum income for non-public assistance families who would be eligible to purchase stamps and the bonus for families already participating, but also raising the cost of the stamps
    B.   *lowering* both the maximum income for non-public assistance families who would be eligible to purchase stamps and the bonus for families already participating, but lowering the cost of the stamps
    C.   *raising* the maximum income for non-public assistance families who would be eligible to purchase stamps and lowering the cost of the stamps, but lowering the bonus for families already participating
    D.   *lowering* the maximum income for non-public assistance families who would be eligible to purchase stamps and raising the cost of the stamps, but also raising the bonus for families already participating

4. The Federal Revenue Act of 1971 included special benefits for working mothers who   4.____
    have child care expenses in that it provides for deduction of

    A.   specific household and child care expenses for single, divorced, or widowed parents only
    B.   specific household and child care expenses for dependents under 15
    C.   carfare and other expenses relevant to the mother's employment
    D.   allowance for an additional dependent for the person caring for the child

5. A SERIOUS objection raised by those who considered a proposal for revenue sharing by the Federal government to be a major threat to welfare reform is that

   A. states and localities would not have sufficient control over how the money is spent
   B. increased state and local control over expenditures had consistently worked against disadvantaged and minority groups
   C. there are no Federal provisions for enforcement of compliance with regard to discrimination for reason of race, color, or national origin
   D. the state governors would not be able to set their own priorities or monitor violations by local officials

6. Of the following, the SMALLEST number of recipients of public assistance consists of

   A. children under 21   B. aged adults
   C. employables   D. adults caring for others

7. Responsibility for quality control studies of public assistance clients' eligibility in the city by means of interviews and analysis of case records has been taken over by the

   A. U.S. Department of Health, Education and Welfare
   B. State Department of Social Services
   C. City Department of Investigation
   D. Bureau of Income Maintenance of the Human Resources Administration

8. The one of the following which is NOT a current method being used by the human services agency in its efforts to reduce welfare costs is

   A. improvement of managerial capability
   B. simplification of procedures
   C. insistence on greater accountability
   D. full investigation of all applicants for assistance

9. The one of the following which would be MOST likely to reduce the tendency of the unemployed poor to migrate to urban centers is

   A. increased federal subsidies to the small farmer
   B. unionization of migrant farm workers
   C. a national guaranteed income maintenance program
   D. an increase in the national minimum wage

10. According to the U.S. Census Bureau Report, economic and educational gains made between 1970 and 1980 by Puerto Ricans living in the city, as compared with Blacks, were

    A. considerably greater   B. considerably smaller
    C. about the same   D. slightly greater

11. Of the following, modern child care experts would consider the LEAST desirable setting for treatment of most juvenile offenders while under professional supervision to be

    A. the family's home   B. a group residence
    C. a foster home   D. a large institution

12. The state has instituted a program of *work relief,* which requires all Home Relief recipients who are eligible to work but cannot find jobs, to *work off* their welfare checks on non-salaried work projects.
    This approach has met with considerable opposition MAINLY because those who oppose it believe that the recipients

    12.____

    A. may take away jobs which were formerly performed by paid employees
    B. are unskilled and therefore qualified for an extremely limited number of work assignments
    C. are likely to be resentful and inefficient in carrying out their assignments
    D. will receive no improvement in financial status and no assurance of stable employment so that they can be removed from the welfare rolls

13. A significant aspect of an amendment to the Social Security Act which became effective recently is that it introduces into the Act a program of

    13.____

    A. public service jobs
    B. income maintenance
    C. medical assistance to the aged
    D. aid to dependent children

14. During the past few years, the U.S. Supreme Court has made a series of key rulings that directly affect welfare clients.
    NONE of these rulings has been concerned with

    14.____

    A. fair hearings
    B. state residence requirements
    C. home inspections
    D. the family assistance plan

15. A demonstration program for public assistance recipients in the city approved by the U.S. Department of Health, Education, and Welfare which has been the subject of considerable controversy is the

    15.____

    A. Incentives for Independence Program
    B. Haitian Training Project
    C. Work Incentive Program
    D. Demonstration Work Project

16. The component of the human services agency which is authorized by the Mayor as the agency to receive community action funds from the Federal government is the

    16.____

    A. Council Against Poverty
    B. Community Development Agency
    C. Manpower and Career Development Agency
    D. Agency for Child Development

17. The Equal Employment Opportunity Commission is CORRECTLY described as the

    17.____

    A. Federal agency which acts on charges of discrimination in employment
    B. state agency which operates employment and specialized placement offices
    C. city agency which develops job opportunities for underemployed persons
    D. city agency which acts on charges of discrimination in employment

18. The reorganization of the Youth Services Agency emphasized administrative changes that would allow for

    A. expansion of counseling, psychological, and psychiatric services to anti-social youth
    B. greater community responsibility for and participation in the delivery of services to parents
    C. more emphasis on direct services to street youth and fighting gangs
    D. establishment of youth narcotics addiction prevention and treatment programs

18.____

19. The BASIC reason for the establishment of the Agency for Child Development as part of the human services agency was to

    A. provide a single agency to consolidate and administe programs for pre-school-age children
    B. establish a commission to insure maximum parent and community involvement in programs for children
    C. take over the licensing of both public and private programs for pre-school-age children
    D. insure a diversity of programs to meet the needs of a broad spectrum of children

19.____

20. The MAIN functions of the Manpower and Career Development Agency (MCDA) are to

    A. run manpower and recruitment centers under contract with private organizations
    B. train the unskilled, upgrade existing skills, develop job opportunities, and place newly-trained people in jobs
    C. provide remedial education and follow-up for disadvan-taged potential college students, vocational counseling and testing for veterans and ex-addicts
    D. provide job development, interviewing and placement, and manpower research services

20.____

Questions 21-25.

DIRECTIONS: Questions 21 through 25 are to be answered SOLELY on the basis of the following paragraph.

    With the generation gap yawning before us, it is well to remember that 20 years ago teenagers produced a larger proportion of unwedlock births than today and that the illegitimacy rate among teenagers is lower than among women in their twenties and thirties. In addition, the illegitimacy rate has risen less among teenagers than among older women.

    It is helpful to note the difference between illegitimacy rate and illegitimacy ratio. The ratio is the number of illegitimate babies per 1,000 live births. The rate is the number of illegitimate births per 1,000 unmarried women of childbearing age. The ratio talks about babies; the rate talks about mothers. The ratio is useful for planning services, but worse than useless for considering trends since it depends on the age and marital <u>composition</u> of the population, illegitimacy rate, and the fertility of married women. For example, the ratio among girls under 18 is bound to be high in comparison with older women since few are married mothers. However, the illegitimacy rate is relatively low.

21. Of the following, the MOST suitable title for the above passage would be: 21.____

    A. The Generation Gap
    B. Moral Standards and Teenage Illegitimacy Ratio
    C. A Comparison of Illegitimacy Rate and Illegitimacy Ratio
    D. Causes of High Illegitimacy Rates

22. According to the above passage, which of the following statements is CORRECT? 22.____
The illegitimacy

    A. rate has fallen among women in their thirties
    B. ratio is the number of illegitimate births per 1,000 unmarried women of childbear-
ing age
    C. ratio is partially dependent on the illegitimacy rate
    D. rate is more useful than the ratio for planning services

23. According to the above passage, of the following age groups, the illegitimacy ratio would 23.____
be expected to be HIGHEST in comparison with the other groups for the group aged

    A. 17   B. 21   C. 25   D. 29

24. According to the above passage, of the following age groups, the illegitimacy rate would 24.____
be expected to be LOWEST in comparison with the other groups for the group aged

    A. 17   B. 21   C. 25   D. 29

25. As used in the above passage, the underlined word *composition* means MOST NEARLY 25.____

    A. essay   B. makeup   C. security   D. happiness

Questions 26-30.

DIRECTIONS: Questions 26 through 30 are to be answered SOLELY on the basis of the following paragraph.

In counting the poor, the Social Security Administration has developed two poverty
thresholds that underline{designate} families as either "poor" or "near poor." The Administration
assumed that the poor would spend the same proportion of income on food as the rest of the
population but that, obviously, since their income was smaller, their range of selection would
be narrower. In the Low Cost Food Plan, the amount underline{allocated to} food from the average
expenditure was cut to the minimum that the Agriculture Department said could still provide
American families with an adequate diet. This Low Cost Food Plan was used to characterize
the "near poor" category, and an even lower Economy Food Plan was used to characterize
the "poor" category. The Economy Food Plan was based on 70 cents a person for food each
day, assuming that all food would be prepared at home. The Agriculture Department esti-
mates that only about 10 percent of persons spending 70 cents or less for food each day
actually were able to get a nutritionally adequate diet.

26. Of the following, the MOST suitable title for the above paragraph would be 26.____

    A. The Superiority of the Economy Plan Over the Low Cost Plan
    B. The Need for a Nutritionally Adequate Diet
    C. Food Expenditures of the Poor and the Near Poor
    D. Diet in the United States

27. According to the above paragraph, the Social Security Administration assumed, in setting its poverty levels, that the poor   27.____

    A.   spend a smaller proportion of income for food than the average non-poor
    B.   would not eat in restaurants
    C.   as a group includes only those with a nutritionally inadequate diet
    D.   spend more money on food than the near poor

28. According to the above paragraph, it would be CORRECT to state that the Low Cost Food Plan   28.____

    A.   is above the minimum set by the Agriculture Department for a nutritionally adequate diet
    B.   gives most people a nutritionally inadequate diet
    C.   is lower than the Economy Food Plan
    D.   represents the amount spent by the near poor

29. As estimated by the Department of Agriculture, the percentage of people spending 70 cents or less a day for food who did NOT get a nutritionally adequate diet was   29.____

    A.   100%   B.   90%   C.   10%   D.   0%

30. As used in the above paragraph, the underlined words *allocated to* mean MOST NEARLY   30.____

    A.   offered for   B.   assigned to
    C.   wasted on   D.   spent on

Questions 31-35.

DIRECTIONS: Questions 31 through 35 are to be answered SOLELY on the basis of the following graphs. Note that the unemployment rate for employables who move into Central City is the same as for the City as a whole.

EMPLOYABLES
IN THOUSANDS

EMPLOYABLES WHO MOVED INTO CENTRAL CITY
1970-1981

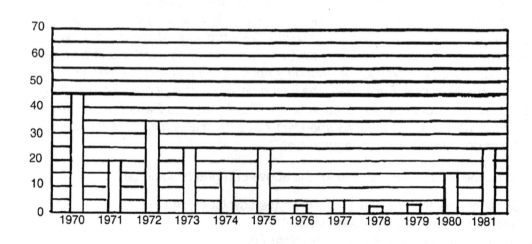

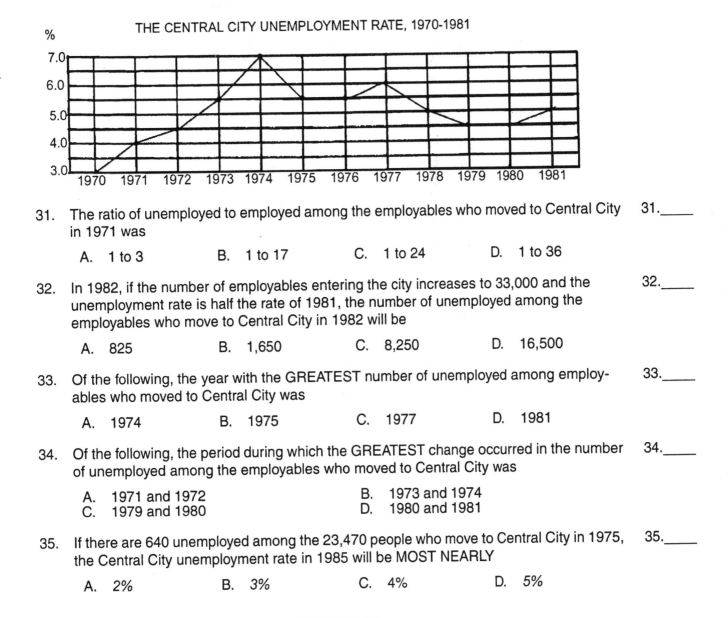

THE CENTRAL CITY UNEMPLOYMENT RATE, 1970-1981

31. The ratio of unemployed to employed among the employables who moved to Central City   31.____
in 1971 was

    A. 1 to 3   B. 1 to 17   C. 1 to 24   D. 1 to 36

32. In 1982, if the number of employables entering the city increases to 33,000 and the   32.____
unemployment rate is half the rate of 1981, the number of unemployed among the
employables who move to Central City in 1982 will be

    A. 825   B. 1,650   C. 8,250   D. 16,500

33. Of the following, the year with the GREATEST number of unemployed among employ-   33.____
ables who moved to Central City was

    A. 1974   B. 1975   C. 1977   D. 1981

34. Of the following, the period during which the GREATEST change occurred in the number   34.____
of unemployed among the employables who moved to Central City was

    A. 1971 and 1972   B. 1973 and 1974
    C. 1979 and 1980   D. 1980 and 1981

35. If there are 640 unemployed among the 23,470 people who move to Central City in 1975,   35.____
the Central City unemployment rate in 1985 will be MOST NEARLY

    A. 2%   B. 3%   C. 4%   D. 5%

KEY (CORRECT ANSWERS)

1.	B		16.	D
2.	A		17.	A
3.	A		18.	A
4.	B		19.	D
5.	B		20.	B
6.	C		21.	C
7.	B		22.	C
8.	D		23.	A
9.	C		24.	A
10.	B		25.	B
11.	D		26.	C
12.	D		27.	B
13.	A		28.	D
14.	D		29.	B
15.	A		30.	B

31.	C
32.	A
33.	B
34.	A
35.	B

EXAMINATION SECTION
TEST 1

DIRECTIONS: Each question or incomplete statement is followed by several suggested answers or completions. Select the one that BEST answers the question or completes the statement. *PRINT THE LETTER OF THE CORRECT ANSWER IN THE SPACE AT THE RIGHT.*

1. The one of the following which would NOT be an appropriate means of ensuring effective community and client participation in program planning and development is

    A. the establishment of citizen advisory committees which include welfare recipients

    B. employment of indigenous community service aides, including recipients

    C. development of appeal and grievance machinery to give client groups access to the administration of the agency

    D. negotiations with staff employee organizations on matters of agency programs

1.____

2. Representatives of a community organization which has an interest in developing a narcotics service program in a neighborhood with a high rate of narcotics addiction meet with the director of the social services center in order to ask for assistance in developing this program

The MOST appropriate action for the director to take FIRST would be to

    A. assign a staff member to work with the group

    B. inform the group that development of narcotics service programs is not a responsibility of the Department of Social Services

    C. ask your superior to send a consultant to meet with you in order to develop a plan

    D. inform the group that you cannot refer the matter to the Addiction Services Agency since it is not their responsibility

2.____

3. Assume that the Department of Social Services has decided to organize local groups to assist in informing the communities of the availability and the nature of services provided under separation of income maintenance from delivery of social services.

The one of the following which would NOT be an appropriate step to take in order to organize such community groups is to

    A. call a meeting of the representatives of existing community agencies in order to form an advisory committee

    B. ask the neighborhood urban task force to suggest suitable community residents for membership in these groups

    C. make a study in order to obtain relevant facts about the community

    D. identify the informal community power structure

3.____

4. As a result of a study, private casework Agency X, which has a large center serving your geographical area, has decided to de-emphasize social casework and move into neighborhood organization.
    As director of the social services center, the MOST appropriate action for you to take FIRST in order to cooperate with this agency's new program would be
    A. offer to take over the caseload and provide the social services
    B. set up a meeting with the professional leadership of the agency to discuss implications and possible transition of clients into available services
    C. convene the local citizen advisory group and get their reaction to Agency X's decision
    D. purchase casework services for the welfare clients formerly served by Agency X from other voluntary agencies

4.____

5. *America's families are in trouble – trouble so deep and pervasive as to threaten the future of our nation*, according to a major report to the White House Conference on Children. Conference participants agreed generally that family life is being weakened by various fundamental changes in American citizens. Many experts believe that the ONLY remaining function that justifies continued support of the family as a social institution is its function as a
    A. medium for the education of children
    B. source of emotional security for family members
    C. means of day-to-day care of children
    D. vehicle for the socialization of its members

5.____

6. The administration's proposed Family Assistance Plan was applauded in some quarters because it established the principle of a guaranteed annual income for all Americans. However, many social welfare experts who otherwise favor the guaranteed income principle have voiced criticism of this part of the proposed plan because the
    A. proposed amount of the income guarantee was lower in many states than present welfare benefits
    B. income guarantee was not tied in with a provision that recipients of the guaranteed income are required to work
    C. proposed guaranteed income plan does not consider family composition and family size
    D. lots of welfare recipients in those states which already have comparatively high welfare benefits would have been improved further

6.____

7. The Federal Task Force on the Organization of the Social Services has summed up some major principles which should be guidelines in revising the service aspect of the Department of Social Services.
    The one of the following which is NOT one of these principles is:
    A. The federal government should assume the entire burden of income maintenance
    B. Consumers should be involved in the planning of services
    C. Services should be directed only to those who are poor or are in danger of becoming poor and eligible for income maintenance
    D. States and local communities should have the option of developing their own style and package of services

7.____

8. According to a recent five-year study, the rate of illegitimate births in the
   United States has nearly doubled during the last decade.
   Of the following, the MOST correct statement about the findings on this
   problem is that
   A. the basic cause of this increase in the rate of illegitimate births could not
      be determined
   B. a direct link was found between illegitimacy rates and the number of
      families receiving welfare benefits
   C. illegitimacy rates were found to be highest in those states with high
      welfare benefits and lowest in those states with low welfare benefits
   D. there is a significant relationship between inadequate sex education in
      schools and the rate of illegitimate motherhood among school-age young
      women

8.____

9. Congressional statutes have extended the Food Stamp program, introducing
   various changes and policy revisions.
   A SIGNIFICANT change made by Congress is that
   A. college students are ineligible to receive food stamps
   B. recipients of public assistance to not have the option of paying for their
      food stamps by means of an authorized deduction in their public
      assistance grant
   C. members of hippie communes are eligible to receive food stamps
   D. employable persons who are not already working are required to register
      for and accept work in order to be eligible for food stamps

9.____

10. Under a proposed Family Assistance Program, federal grants would be made
    to the states for individual and family services.
    The one of the following which is a CORRECT statement of the relevant
    provisions of the proposed program is that the states
    A. would be encouraged to provide individual and family services on the
       basis of 75% federal reimbursement for specified services, such as child
       welfare, protective services, family and marriage counseling, and family
       planning
    B. administering the program must be organizationally connected with the
       agency administering a cash benefit program on the basis of need
    C. would not be reimbursed by the federal government for foster care for any
       child for whom a public agency has responsibility
    D. would be discouraged from providing services for low income families
       above the poverty level in order to forestall dependency

10.____

11. The one of the following statements which MOST accurately characterizes
    the social services programs developed during the War Against Poverty is:
    A. Priority was given to the opportunity program (e.g., job training education)
       as contrasted with counseling on personal problems
    B. There was an increasing emphasis on income maintenance programs
    C. There was substantial emphasis on practical or hard social services such
       as Meals on Wheels and homemaker services
    D. There was a substantial emphasis on soft social services such as family
       and interpersonal counseling

11.____

12. The State Legislature adopted the so-called flat grant, which provides for a   12.____
uniform assistance allowance based on family size to meet all needs except for
shelter and which eliminated most special allowances.
The one of the following which has NOT occurred as a result of the adoption of
the flat grant is:
 A. Improved fiscal control over expenditures made for public assistance
 because costs can be predicted more accurately
 B. Significant reduction in underpayments and overpayments in computing
 individual family assistance allowances
 C. Almost no reduction in the number of requests for fair hearings on the
 grounds of inadequacy of the grant
 D. Facilitation of the individual caseworker's job because of the relative ease
 in computing the individual family's allowance

13. As a matter of basic state policy, recipients are required to receive their   13.____
assistance payments in the form of cash. However, it is recognized that under
certain specified circumstances, a grant may be restricted in some manner or
form because of the circumstances involved.
Restriction of the grant would NOT be appropriate in which one of the following
instances?
 A. The cost of care of a recipient's child in a day care center is being met by
 a payment directly to the center
 B. A landlord decides not to evict a recipient who failed to pay his rent
 promptly if he receives subsequent rent payment in the form of a vendor
 payment from the agency
 C. The insurance premiums fall due on a recipient's policy which has been
 assigned to the agency, and the premium is paid directly to the insurance
 company
 D. An aged recipient proves incompetent to handle his money, and
 arrangements are made to have his sister, who lives in the neighborhood,
 receive his check as a protective payee

14. In order to be eligible for matching federal funds, the state's AABD programs   14.____
must conform to certain federal requirements which have been laid down by
the provisions of the Social Security Act.
The one of the following which is NOT included in the Act is the requirement of
 A. training and effective use of paid sub-professional staff, including
 recipients and other persons of low income
 B. training and use of unpaid or partially paid volunteers in the provision of
 services
 C. the use of a simplified statement and method for determining eligibility
 D. separation of income maintenance and service activities into two separate
 organizational units

15. Of the following, the three groups of welfare recipients which were NOT   15.____
affected by recent cutbacks are
    A. dependent children, the aged, and those on home relief
    B. The disabled, dependent children, and the blind
    C. The aged, the blind, and those on home relief
    D. The disabled, the aged, and the blind

16. The adoption of the flat grant system by the State Legislature resulted, in part,   16.____
    A. as a fulfillment of a federal requirement
    B. as a reaction to overutilization by recipients of their entitlement to special
       need items
    C. from a recommendation by the Mayor of the City
    D. from negotiations of the union with the Department of Social Services

17. The problem of developing social planning data has been complicated in the   17.____
city because public agencies have delineated geographic planning or
government areas with different boundaries from those used by voluntary or
quasi-public organizations.
To overcome this problem, the city has proposed planning bases which utilize
geographic areas comprising the _____ districts.
    A. community planning   B. elementary school
    C. health   D. new election

18. The declaration technique as a simplified method of determining eligibility for   18.____
public assistance has resulted in all of the following EXCEPT
    A. a saving of time and manpower previously spent in verifying information
    B. substantial overall personnel budget savings
    C. speedier delivery of financial assistance to the client
    D. enhancement of the dignity of the client

19. Of the following statements, the one which is MOST representative of the DAB   19.____
system now operating in the Department of Social Services under separation of
income maintenance and delivery services is as follows:
    A. It is organized in such a manner as to provide for the same treatment of
       short-term and long-term services needs
    B. It is caseload organized for meeting client service needs
    C. The service needs of recipients are met only on request, except when
       protective services are required
    D. A social study is prepared initially and periodically in order to assess a
       recipient's need for services

KEY (CORRECT ANSWERS)

1.	D	11.	A
2.	A	12.	A
3.	B	13.	A
4.	B	14.	D
5.	B	15.	D
6.	A	16.	B
7.	C	17.	A
8.	A	18.	B
9.	D	19.	C
10.	A		

TEST 2

DIRECTIONS: Each question or incomplete statement is followed by several suggested answers or completions. Select the one that BEST answers the question or completes the statement. *PRINT THE LETTER OF THE CORRECT ANSWER IN THE SPACE AT THE RIGHT.*

1. With regard to the substantial overall rise in the public assistance caseload in the city in recent years, it would be CORRECT to state that the
    A. rise in the caseload was approximately the same for all categories of assistance
    B. AFDC caseload showed the greatest percentage increase
    C. AABD caseload remained at the same level, despite the overall increase
    D. AD caseload showed the greatest percentage of increase

1.____

2. During the last few years, the public assistance caseload in the city has substantially increased.
    According to a study of welfare income and employment in the city, the PRINCIPAL reason for this growth is the
    A. break-up of families due to desertion, separation, and other families
    B. higher ate of acceptance of applications
    C. increase in the number of applications for public assistance
    D. migration of families to the city

2.____

3. There has been considerable debate on alternative methods of giving greater assistance to municipalities because of the rising costs of welfare.
    Many public welfare experts believe that the plan that would be MOST beneficial to the city is
    A. the revenue sharing plan of the administration
    B. the proposal for federalization of DAB and a guaranteed income per family
    C. establishment of a residence requirement to prevent influx of new clients
    D. an increase in the minimum wage

3.____

4. The concept of advocacy of the client as an important function of the public welfare agency and its staff members can BEST be defined by one of the following? A(n)
    A. contribution of advice and support to the client in his dealings with outside agencies
    B. planned expenditure of effort, professional knowledge and skill in the interests of the client
    C. means of providing legal defense for the client in his dealings with the law and the courts
    D. organized effort to advance a public cause or proposal involving client interests

4.____

5. Welfare officials have expressed skepticism about the amount of welfare cost that would be saved as a result of a proposal for a one-year residency requirement.
   According to authorities, of the total number of welfare recipients, those with LESS than one-year residency amount to
       A. 1.5%   B. 3%   C. 5%   D. 7.5%

    5.____

6. Social welfare experts differentiate between the residual and institutional viewpoints as the dominant concepts of social welfare.
   The difference between these concepts can be CORRECTLY described as follows:

    6.____

	Residual Concept	Institutional Concept
A.	Social welfare is a source of supplementary rehabilitative services to be utilized when regular social processes break down.	Social welfare programs are an integral part and legitimate function of modern society.
B.	The provision of social welfare services is an anomalous function no longer applicable to modern industrial society.	Social welfare programs are land established and a necessary function which is essential to modern life.
C.	The financing of social welfare services is a function which should be the responsibility of federal, state, and the local government.	Social welfare services should be financed by private philanthropic institutions.
D.	The provisions of social welfare services is an essential governmental function and the categorical entitlement of citizens.	Social welfare services are a resource to be utilized only when other institutions are unable to provide these services.

7. Lowering income eligibility for Medicaid would PROBABLY result in a(n)
   A. decrease in welfare costs
   B. increase in the number of welfare recipients
   C. loss of matching federal funds
   D. increase in federal funding

    7.____

8. AFDC clients generally had a variety of individual and family problems in addition to financial need which require appropriate services.
   A study of the characteristics of AFDC cases in the state revealed that services other than financial assistance received by the LARGEST number of AFDC clients related to
   A. improvement of home and financial management
   B. establishment of paternity
   C. family planning
   D. referral for work or job training

    8.____

9. The agencies which provide manpower, training, and placement services for public assistance recipients have been severely criticized because of overlapping, poor coordination, and lack of priorities. Suggestions have been made which would eliminate some of these deficiencies.
   Of the following, the MOST widely advocated suggestion is:
   A. All vocational training programs presently the responsibility of DHEW should be transferred to the U.S. Department of Labor
   B. Federal funds should be channeled directly to the larger cities in order to minimize the role of state governments in the allocation of funds
   C. A vast system of public employment should be established in order to make the government the employer of last resort
   D. Welfare recipients should be entitled to a top priority in having job training needs met

9.____

10. In recent years, while labor unions negotiated substantial contract settlements in most sectors of the economy, the occupations which received the LARGEST percentage of gains were in the
    A. clerical and sales categories
    B. construction industry
    C. professional categories
    D. service industries

10.____

11. The requirement of maximum feasible participation of the poor has had a profound influx on anti-poverty programs.
    Of the following, the MOST serious problem in fulfilling this requirement has been the
    A. inability to recruit a sufficient number of welfare recipients and indigenous poor who are interested in and capable of involvement in program planning
    B. difficult task of transforming administration in the delivery of social services to achieve client involvement while losing administrative skill and decisiveness
    C. fact that inexperienced poor participants have had a tendency to take control of the programs out of the hands of interested and skillful professionals
    D. creation of antagonism in the middle class communities by aggressive and militant actions organized by welfare recipients and other poor participants

11.____

12. Job enlargement, a new approach to raising employee interest and increasing efficiency, is characterized by an increase in the variety of tasks performed by an employee.
    The job enlargement approach is designed to
    A. more fully utilize the employee's capabilities, while increasing his responsibilities and according him more freedom of decision
    B. decrease the need for training and for the employee to consult with his peers and superiors
    C. lower the cost of labor and reduce the number of more highly-skilled employees
    D. provide increased employment opportunities for the mentally handicapped and emotionally disturbed

12.____

13. As public social service agencies shift their major focus away from eligibility determination, there is the need to develop new priorities, concepts, and techniques in the delivery of social services.
The one of the following which would NOT be an appropriate aspect of such a program is
   A. decentralization of services
   B. elimination of client information and referral services
   C. client participation in the delivery of services
   D. an interdisciplinary approach in the delivery of services

13.____

14. Although large organizations tend to resist change, an organization is MOST likely to change, according to historical evidence, when
   A. it becomes necessary for survival of the organization
   B. the interests of the community at large are at stake
   C. innovations are recommended and approved by administrators and planners
   D. community groups take part in the planning of services

14.____

15. Studies have shown that most mentally handicapped can be trained for gainful employment.
Generally, MOST of the occupations for which they can be trained are classified as
   A. governmental   B. para-professional
   C. sales and clerical   D. service

15.____

Questions 16-20.

DIRECTIONS: Questions 16 through 20 are to be answered on the basis of the following paragraphs. Based on the information in the paragraphs, mark your answer as follows:
   A. if only statement I is correct
   B. if only statement II is correct
   C. if both statements are correct
   D. if the excerpts do not contain sufficient evidence for concluding whether either or both statements are correct

Almost 49,000 children were living in foster family homes or voluntary institutions in New York State at the end of 2008. These were children whose parents or relatives were unable or unwilling to care for them in their own homes. The New York State Department of Social Services supervised the care of these children served under the auspices of 64 social services districts and more than 150 private agencies and institutions. Almost 8 out of every 1,000 children 18 years of age or younger were in care away from their homes at the end of 2008. This estimate does not include a substantial, but unknown, number of children living outside their own homes who were placed there by their parents, relatives, or others without the assistance of a social agency.

The number of children in care (dependent, neglected, and delinquent combined) was up by 4,500 or 10 percent over the 2005-2008 period. Both New York City and upstate New York reported similar increases. In the comparable period, New York State's child population (18 years or less) rose only three percent. Thus, the foster care rate showed a moderate increase to 7.7 per thousand in 2008 from 7.2 per thousand in 2005. New York City's foster care rate in 2008, at 10.5 per thousand, was almost twice that for upstate New York, 5.7 per thousand. (Excluding delinquent children from the total in care in the state reduces the foster care rate per thousand to 7.2 in 2008 and the comparable 2005 figure to 6.7.)

Dependent and neglected children made up about 95 percent of the total number in foster family homes and voluntary institutions in New York State at the end of 2008, as they did in 2005. Delinquent children sent into care (outside the state training school system) by the Family Court accounted for only 5 percent of the total. The number of delinquent children in care rose 5 percent, as an increase in upstate New York. 28 percent more than offset a 13 percent decline in New York City. Delinquents comprised 4.9 percent of the total number of children in care upstate at the end of 2008 and 3.9 percent in New York City.

16. I.   There were 45,000 children in care away from their own homes over the 2005-2008 period.
     II. The percentage decline of delinquent children in care in New York City in 2008 was offset by a greater increase in the rest of the state.
     The CORRECT answer is:
     A. A   B. B   C. C   D. D

16.____

17. I.   The increase in delinquent care rate in New York State from 2005 to 2008 cannot be determined from the data given.
     II. New York State's foster care rate in 2008, exclusive of New York City, was about one-half the rate for New York City.
     The CORRECT answer is:
     A. A   B. B   C. C   D. D

17.____

18. I.   In 2005 and 2008, the percentage of dependent and neglected children in foster family homes and voluntary institutions in New York State was about the same.
     II. In 2005, the number of dependent and neglected children in foster family homes and voluntary institutions in New York State was 43,250.
     The CORRECT answer is:
     A. A   B. B   C. C   D. D

18.____

19. I.   New York City's child population rose approximately three percent from 2005 to 2008.
     II. At the end of 2008, less than 1% of the children 18 years of age or younger were in care.
     The CORRECT answer is:
     A. A   B. B   C. C   D. D

19.____

20. I.   Delinquents in New York City comprised 4.4 percent of the total number
          of children in care in New York City at the end of 2005.
    II.   An unsubstantial number of children living outside their own homes were
          placed by their parents or relatives without the assistance of a social
          agency.
    The CORRECT answer is:
    A. A   B. B   C. C   D. D

20.____

―――――――

KEY (CORRECT ANSWERS)

1.	D	11.	A
2.	C	12.	A
3.	B	13.	B
4.	B	14.	A
5.	A	15.	D
6.	A	16.	B
7.	B	17.	B
8.	A	18.	A
9.	B	19.	D
10.	B	20.	D

―――――――

EXAMINATION SECTION
TEST 1

DIRECTIONS: Each question or incomplete statement is followed by several suggested answers or completions. Select the one that BEST answers the question or completes the statement. *PRINT THE LETTER OF THE CORRECT ANSWER IN THE SPACE AT THE RIGHT.*

1. In recent years, the social work profession has shifted in emphasis from concern with individual adjustment to concentration on environmental change.
   The one of the following which has NOT generally accompanied this change of emphasis is the

   A. development of new roles for social work professionals
   B. employment of non-professionals in human service organizations
   C. growth of citizen participation in social service programs
   D. determination of the community's appropriate role in relation to the agency's stage of development

   1._____

2. The reporting system known as the Social Services Information System (SSIS) is BEST described as a method of

   A. determining how direct-service staff allocate their time in relation to defined productivity measures and operating costs
   B. defining the work of a public social service agency in terms of services, elements, activities, and costs
   C. evaluating performance of staff in terms of how they allocate their time in relation to defined productivity measures
   D. determining costs for individual cases in terms of how staff allocate their time to related services, elements, and activities

   2._____

3. The one of the following which is NOT a major purpose of the Social Services Information System (SSIS) is the provision of information useful in determining

   A. trends in clientele
   B. quality of service
   C. shifts in service demands
   D. service priorities

   3._____

4. The system of reporting delivery of services under Goal-Oriented Social Services (GOSS) DIFFERS from the reporting requirements introduced by the 1962 Social Security amendments in that the focus of GOSS is in the

   A. objectives of specific areas of services delivery
   B. service plan for the client and the overall, long-term case purpose
   C. allocation of resources
   D. objectives set by the caseworker rather than the client

   4._____

5. In the language of social service programming, case accountability means MOST NEARLY

   A. departmental responsibility for costs of all services provided for children, adult clients, and families
   B. continuing responsibility for service to a family until the case is closed

   5._____

C. organizational autonomy for those services the particular organization provides for children, adults, and families
D. departmental responsibility to the consumer and the public for providing needed services

6. After years of controversy, family planning services are now being supported by sound fiscal backing and federal mandate.
According to current requirements, family planning services must be made available to ALL

    6._____

A. persons requesting such services
B. persons 14 years of age and over
C. female heads of households
D. women of child-bearing age

7. Research studies indicate that, of the following, the basic strength of a community program sponsored by a public or voluntary agency depends MOST directly on the

A. enlistment of support from representative minority community leaders

    7._____

B. degree of understanding by professional community organization workers of the life-style of community residents
C. ability of community organization workers to help disadvantaged community members develop their feelings of self-worth
D. complete control by indigenous people of decision-making and operation of the program

8. Which of the following developments would have the MOST significant impact on the current trend toward decentralization in the delivery of social services?

    8._____

A. Action by the U.S. Congress which would reduce the number of federally mandated social services
B. Takeover by the State Department of Social Services of some aspects of the medical assistance program
C. Participation by the Community Development Agency with the Department of Social Services in planning for community social services
D. amendments to the Social Security Act assigning responsibility to the states for definition of services, eligibility standards, and regulations

9. When the AFDC mother's youngest child becomes eighteen, the mother is no longer eligible to receive AFDC benefits. A problem equal in magnitude to the problems of job scarcity and lack of training opportunities is the unreadiness of some of these women to move into the competitive labor market.
The one of the following which would be the MOST appropriate suggestion to help increase the motivation of AFDC mothers to become self-dependent is the establishment of

    9._____

A. cash stipends to AFDC mothers who participate in training programs
B. therapeutic groups to help AFDC mothers develop confidence and self-esteem
C. a food stamp bonus system for AFDC mothers who accept job offers
D. special community-based centers for individual job counselling of AFDC mothers

10. The one of the following which is NOT generally considered to be a function of the community social worker is to

    A. act as a catalyst for the organization or community groups
    B. provide leadership in identifying community needs
    C. arrange group programs such as group counselling and consumer education
    D. give *in-depth* casework service to community residents

10._____

11. Of the following, the OLDEST original model for social work practice is

    A. group treatment
    B. milieu therapy
    C. task and situational strategy
    D. social diagnosis

11._____

12. The term *diagnosis,* as used in social work, USUALLY refers to the worker's
    A. professional assessment as to the nature of the need or the problem which the client presents
    B. identification of mental illness by investigation of its symptoms and its history
    C. recommendation as to the treatment plan for the client on the basis of his problems
    D. categorization of the individual client according to a functional classification of psycho-social problems

12._____

13. The aim of crisis intervention and treatment as a model of social work practice is to
    A. give the most help to individuals who view a crisis as a challenge rather than a threat
    B. restore the person to the level of functioning he was able to reach before the crisis occurred, and help him achieve more effective functioning if possible
    C. assess the state of crisis and the person's capacity to cope with the situation
    D. make an objective determination of the reality of the crisis in terms of the person's life situation in order to help him develop new adaptive mechanisms

13._____

14. The traditional unit of attention in social casework has been the

    A. client's environment and economic situation
    B. person-in-situation configuration
    C. opportunity systems available to the client
    D. person's ability to overcome his problems

14._____

15. The one of the following which is GENERALLY considered to be a basic purpose of the separation of income maintenance and social services is to

    A. maximize the client's choices and control over his own affairs
    B. establish more efficient methods of eligibility determination
    C. encourage community participation in the delivery of social services
    D. reduce the need for workers with college degrees and professional social work training

15._____

16. The current Federal effort to retrench on the funding of social services is accompanied by considerable debate over the merits of *hard* vs. *soft* services.
The one of the following which can be classified as a *soft* service is

    A. child care for working mothers
    B. family planning
    C. physical therapy
    D. rehabilitation

16._____

17. Social work profession has developed in a pattern that is quite different from other professions in that the emphasis in social work practice has changed from _____ to _____.

    A. generalist; specialist   B. specialist; generalist
    C. activist; reformer   D. counselor; therapist

17.___

18. Senior citizens require a variety of services to enable them to cope effectively with physical and psychological changes and the loss of social contacts.
Of the following services, senior citizen centers can be MOST useful for providing elderly clients with

    A. protective care
    B. vocational therapy
    C. health services and nutrition education
    D. new identifications, roles, and relationships

18.___

19. Services to alcoholics and drug abusers have been expanded to include many different types of treatment modalities. However, experts generally agree that an ESSENTIAL element of any successful treatment plan is

    A. psychoactive medication
    B. deterrent therapy
    C. individual and/or group counselling
    D. family counselling

19.___

20. Protective services in child abuse cases are now directed towards improving and strengthening positive functioning in the child's own family in order to avoid the destructive effects of separation of the child from the family. Which of the following treatment modalities would offer the GREATEST potential for success in achieving this objective?

    A. Frequent regular psychotherapy sessions for the abusing parent while the child remains at home
    B. Family counselling of the parents and siblings while the child is temporarily placed in foster care
    C. Daytime child care services for the abused child, combined with therapeutic group services for the parents
    D. Admission of the abused child to a day care center and regular psychiatric treatment of the abusing parent

20.___

21. A recent study of multi-problem families on public assistance in the city of Baltimore gives evidence that individuals and families who are most seriously in need of social services are least likely to take the initiative to ask for services.
Of the following services, this finding has the MOST significant implications for the current public welfare policy and practice of

    A. goal-oriented social services
    B. separation of income maintenance and social services
    C. decentralization of service delivery
    D. work relief employment services

21.___

22. The State Task Force on Welfare and Social Services, known as the Scott Commission, focused PRIMARILY on the

    A. administration of financial assistance
    B. delivery of social services
    C. elimination of welfare fraud
    D. State take-over of income support operations

23. Separation of the income maintenance and social services functions originated from action by the

    A. U.S. Congress
    B. State Department of Social Services
    C. U.S. Department of Health, Education and Welfare
    D. Human Resources Administration

24. The supervisor should be familiar with many statutes, rules, and regulations for administration of care of children at public expense.
Which of the following would be LEAST relevant to his work?

    A. Social Welfare Law
    B. Rules and Regulations of H.E.W.
    C. Rules and Regulations of the State Board and State Department of Social Services
    D. The Family Court Act of NY State

25. Assume that a supervisor is reviewing a sample of case records in order to evaluate the effectiveness of his subordinates' service to clients.
Of the following, the BEST indication that a worker is making effective referrals of clients to other community agencies would be when the case record shows that the

    A. client has participated in the decision to make the contact with the other agency
    B. caseworker has no further contact with the other agency after the initial referral
    C. client has no further contact with the caseworker after keeping his appointment with the other agency
    D. caseworker visits the other agency before making referrals

---

KEY (CORRECT ANSWERS)

1.	D		11.	D
2.	A		12.	A
3.	B		13.	B
4.	B		14.	B
5.	B		15.	A
6.	B		16.	C
7.	C		17.	B
8.	D		18.	D
9.	B		19.	C
10.	D		20.	C

21. B
22. B
23. C
24. B
25. A

TEST 2

DIRECTIONS: Each question or incomplete statement is followed by several suggested
answers or completions. Select the one that BEST answers the question or
completes the statement. *PRINT THE LETTER OF THE CORRECT ANSWER
IN THE SPACE AT THE RIGHT.*

1. Of the following, a SIGNIFICANT criticism recently made of the separation of income
   maintenance and social services is that services are separated without

   A. requiring periodic diagnosis of clients' problems
   B. directing clients to accept services
   C. offering referrals to private agencies
   D. making clients responsible for recognizing their needs for services

   1._____

2. The MAIN source of the salaries of public assistance clients who are placed in city jobs
   through the Work Relief Employment Program is

   A. city capital budget funds   C. state appropriations
   B. federal appropriations   D. welfare funds

   2._____

3. Photo ID cards, required for public assistance recipients by State regulations, were
   INITIALLY proposed for the purpose of

   A. locating ineligibles   C. recertification of clients
   B. protecting clients   D. reducing case load growth

   3._____

4. A significant aspect of the general revenue sharing bill (P.L. 92-512) which has a direct
   impact on the expansion of social services programs is the tendency of this legislation to

   A. shift decision-making authority to states and localities and reduce federal responsi-
      bility for solutions to economic and social problems
   B. give states and localities unrestricted use of revenue-sharing funds for expendi-
      tures without considering specified priority areas
   C. give the federal government tighter control over revenue-sharing funds used to
      establish and expand social service programs
   D. allocate decision-making authority to states and localities on the basis of popula-
      tion as indicated by census figures

   4._____

5. Which of the following is a present trend in community social services for the disadvantaged concurrent with the separation of income maintenance and social services?

   A. Emphasis on family functioning
   B. Lowered status of the social work professional
   C. Differential use of income maintenance staff
   D. Elimination of eligibility verification

   5._____

6. The Office of the Welfare Inspector-General, which was established in response to criticism of the efficiency of state and local operations in public assistance eligibility determi-
   nations, was assigned the function of

   A. quality control of eligibility decisions
   B. registry and location of deserting parents
   C. investigation of fraud in local center operations
   D. welfare check reconciliation

   6._____

7. The food stamp program, which was designed to help increase the purchasing power of   7._____
low-income persons, has been only minimally used by those whom it is supposed to ben-
efit.
The one of the following which is NOT a plausible reason for the present underutiliza-
tion of food stamps is that
   A. low-income people do not understand the program or the benefits of the bonus
      system
   B. the recipient's neighbors, store clerks, and casual acquaintances have the opport-
      unity to know that they are getting government aid
   C. information about the program is channeled through institutional sources to the
      largest number of people who use the program
   D. participation is discouraged because of the cumbersome administrative structure
      of the food stamp distribution system

8. State and city public welfare officials have instituted several new administrative proce-   8._____
dures in their efforts to insure the eligibility of the ADC caseload.
Which of the following is NOT one of these procedures?

   A. Face-to-face recertification
   B. Photo identification cards
   C. Mandatory registration with the state employment service
   D. Mailings to verify current address and eligibility status

9. A major organizational change became effective during the seventies, when responsibil-   9._____
ity for financial aid to disabled, aged, and blind clients was transferred from the Human
Resources Administration to the Social Security Administration.
Which of the following responsibilities to DAB clients continues to be carried out by the
Human Resources Administration?

   A. Eligibility certification   B. Provision of social services
   C. Medical assistance   D. Special grants

10. Of the following, the MOST serious problem that has developed as a result of the   10._____
changeover to the Federal Supplemental Security Income program for the aged and
disabled is the

   A. reduction of income for many aged recipients
   B. breakdown between income maintenance and services within the SSI formula
   C. required provision of social services to disabled recipients
   D. disqualification of alcoholics and drug addicts as *disabled* persons eligible for
      benefits

11. The effect of the recent increase in Social Security benefits on aged recipients of the   11._____
Supplemental Security Income program has been to

   A. increase their net benefits
   B. leave their net benefits unchanged.
   C. increase benefits for those who are disabled
   D. raise their support levels

12. United States Supreme Court decisions regarding welfare rights, Jefferson vs. Hackney   12._____
    (1972) and Rosado vs. Wyman (1970), were IMPORTANT cases for comparison
    because both cases deal with the

    A. *substitute father* rule
    B. cost of living provision
    C. residence requirement
    D. mandatory home visits provision

13. The lawsuit, Wilder vs. Sugarman, alleged that the existing statutory base for the   13._____
    provision of child welfare services in New York City is unconstitutional. The suit sought
    to obtain a court order forcing the government agencies named in the petition to develop
    a plan for a new system of publicly supported child-welfare services to meet the present-
    day needs of children and families. The BASIC issue involved in this case is

    A. direct vs. purchased services for children in need of placement
    B. discrimination against black children by private adoption agencies
    C. the requirement of child placement according to race
    D. discrimination against black children in need of services

14. A recent article in a professional journal reported that narcotics addicts make up 10 per-   14._____
    cent of the welfare population, yet account for fully 50 percent of all transactions in the
    centers. The one of the following which is NOT a plausible reason for this situation is that

    A. services to narcotics addicts are more difficult and time-consuming than services
       to other clients
    B. narcotics addicts must be served by selecting a group of specially trained workers
    C. workers must devote more time to medical and psychiatric referrals for narcotics
       addicts
    D. necessary investigation of criminal activity of narcotics addicts is lengthy and
       difficult

15. The incremental approach has recently been discussed in the press as a preferable   15._____
    strategy for welfare reform at this period in history.
    The one of the following which is NOT an example of the incremental approach to
    welfare reform is the

    A. addition of a housing allowance for low-income persons and the use of this new
       benefit as the key to improvement of other programs
    B. provision of a work bonus to effect program reform and integration
    C. introduction of a negative income tax and a comprehensive new welfare program
       to replace most existing programs
    D. expansion of food stamp benefits and addition of a cost-of-living escalation
       provision

16. Of the following, generally the MOST crucial factor which may limit or prevent community   16._____
    participation in social service programs for the disadvantaged is the

    A. middle-class citizen's fear of reinforcing corrupt lifestyles
    B. taxpayers' demands for greater government economy and efficiency
    C. depersonalization and categorization of public assistance clients
    D. inherent inequality between the social work professional and the client

17. Administrators of social programs are in general agreement that public participation is a   17.____
practical and necessary part of the effective implementation of social policy.
In order to ensure optimum public participation in making decisions on the size of public
assistance allotments, it would be PARTICULARLY important to

    A.   allow a majority of the organized welfare recipients to determine the size of the
allotments
    B.   achieve the proper combination of checks and balances among the various
segments of the population relevant to the decision on the size of the allotments
    C.   provide for ongoing, continuous decision-making on public assistance allotments
by the taxpaying public who finance these payments
    D.   make official liaison, concurrence, consultation, and policy-making the
responsibilities of the client population

18. Effective community participation to ensure social justice for minorities does not flow   18.____
automatically from more or maximum participation of individuals.
Of the following, this statement implies MOST NEARLY that

    A.   effective participation requires both professional leadership and numerical strength
    B.   democratic participation is not synonymous with majority rule
    C.   effective participation is determined by the number of decisions made
    D.   majority rule is the best means of obtaining social justice for minority groups

19. Experts generally agree that decisions on the social services to be minimally provided   19.____
must be the result of city-wide centralized coordinated planning by a joint council with
public, voluntary agency and community representation.
The one of the following which would NOT be a desirable result of such coordinated
effort is

    A.   avoidance of gaps and duplication of services
    B.   universality of essential and mandated services
    C.   uniformity of services at the community level
    D.   minimal waste of resources

20. The one of the following elements which is MOST crucial to the success of a community   20.____
social services operation is

    A.   the employment of indigenous paraprofessionals
    B.   operation of a day care service on the premises
    C.   a carefully developed intake process
    D.   centralized preliminary screening unit

21. Questions have been raised about the popular assumption that the special advantage   21.____
of employing indigenous paraprofessionals in social work and mental health agencies is
their similarity in background and abilities to the clients of the agency.
The BASIS for questioning this assumption is the finding that community people who
serve as paraprofessionals

    A.   tend to be better educated, more successful, and more upwardly mobile than their
neighbors
    B.   are unable to be objective about their neighbors' situation and needs because of the
similarity to their own problems
    C.   are more likely to be naive and to allow themselves to be manipulated by the clients
    D.   tend to have inadequate education and lack of ambition and aspiration

22. The Human Resources Administration has a commitment to make extensive use of   22._____
voluntary and community-based organizations as contractors to provide services to clients.
One of the characteristics of a *voluntary*, in contrast to a *community-based* organization,
is that a *voluntary* organization is

     A.   administered mainly by professionally-trained staff
     B.   sponsored and staffed mainly by volunteers
     C.   sponsored by community residents and staffed mainly by non-professionals
     D.   established mainly by means of public funding

23. Decentralization of services into the neighborhoods has been a key feature of the organi-   23._____
zation of the Human Resources Administration during the past few years. However, the
need has recently emerged for a kind of agency which can provide services most
effectively on a city-wide, rather than a neighborhood, basis for

     A.   persons recently discharged from state institutions
     B.   members of other ethnic groups residing in areas largely populated by blacks
     C.   middle-class residents of Human Resources Districts eligible for child welfare
         services
     D.   narcotics addicts

24. A basic problem in the reorganization of the Department of Social Services for separation   24._____
of income maintenance and service functions has been providing access to the service
system.
Which of the following would probably be the MOST productive means of encouraging
clients to use available social services?

     A.   Outreach activities by the Community Development Agency
     B.   Referrals from income maintenance workers
     C.   Referrals from other public and private agencies
     D.   Neighborhood-based information and referral centers

25. Of the following, the MOST crucial step in clarifying long-range community strategy to   25._____
develop coordinated public and privately sponsored social services should be

     A.   emphasis on functions rather than agencies
     B.   definition of the functions of individual agencies
     C.   limitation of the functions of a given agency
     D.   community assignment of functions to each agency

KEY (CORRECT ANSWERS)

1.	A		11.	B
2.	D		12.	B
3.	B		13.	D
4.	A		14.	B
5.	A		15.	C
6.	C		16.	B
7.	C		17.	B
8.	C		18.	B
9.	B		19.	C
10.	B		20.	C

21.	A
22.	A
23.	B
24.	D
25.	A

———

EXAMINATION SECTION
TEST 1

DIRECTIONS: Each question or incomplete statement is followed by several suggested answers or completions. Select the one that BEST answers the question or completes the statement. *PRINT THE LETTER OF IN THE CORRECT ANSWER THE SPACE AT THE RIGHT.*

1. Reports show that more men than women are physically handicapped MAINLY because   1.____

     A. women are instinctively more cautious than men
     B. men are more likely to have congenital deformities
     C. women tend to seek surgical remedies because of greater concern over personal appearance
     D. men have lower ability to recover from injury
     E. men are more likely to be exposed to hazardous conditions

2. Of the following, the explanation married women give MOST frequently for seeking employment outside the home is that they wish to   2.____

     A. escape the drudgeries of home life
     B. develop secondary employment skills
     C. maintain an emotionally satisfying career
     D. provide the main support for the family
     E. supplement the family income

3. Of the following home conditions, the one *most likely* to cause emotional disturbances in children is   3.____

     A. increased birthrate following the war
     B. disrupted family relationships
     C. lower family income than that of neighbors
     D. higher family income than that of neighbors
     E. overcrowded living conditions

4. Casual unemployment, as distinguished from other types of unemployment, is traceable MOST readily to   4.____

     A. a decrease in the demand for labor as a result of scientific progress
     B. more or less haphazard changes in the demand for labor in certain industries
     C. periodic changes in the demand for labor in certain industries
     D. disturbances and disruptions in industry resulting from international trade barriers
     E. increased mobility of the population

5. Labor legislation, although primarily intended for the benefit of the employee, MAY aid the employer by   5.____

     A. increasing his control over the immediate labor market
     B. prohibiting government interference with operating policies
     C. protecting him, through equalization of labor costs, from being undercut by other employers
     D. transferring to the general taxpayer the principal costs of industrial hazards of accident and unemployment
     E. increasing the pensions of civil service employees

6. When employment and unemployment figures both decline, the MOST probable conclu- 6._____
sion is that

    A. the population has reached a condition of equilibrium
    B. seasonal employment has ended
    C. the labor force has decreased
    D. payments for unemployment insurance have been increased
    E. industrial progress has reduced working hours

7. An individual with an I.Q. of 100 may be said to have demonstrated _____ intelligence. 7._____

    A. superior
    B. absolute
    C. substandard
    D. approximately average
    E. high average

8. While state legislatures differ in many respects, all of them are *most nearly* alike in 8._____

    A. provisions for retirement of members
    B. rate of pay
    C. length of legislative sessions
    D. method of selection of their members
    E. length of term of office

9. If a state passed a law in a field under Congressional jurisdiction and if Congress subse- 9._____
quently passed contrary legislation, the state provision would be

    A. regarded as never having existed
    B. valid until the next session of the state legislature, which would be obliged to repeal
       it
    C. superseded by the federal statute
    D. ratified by Congress
    E. still operative in the state involved

10. Power to pardon offenses committed against the people of the United States is vested in 10._____
the

    A. Supreme Court of the United States
    B. United States District Courts
    C. Federal Bureau of Investigation
    D. United States Parole Board
    E. President of the United States

11. As distinguished from formal social control of an individual's behavior, an example of 11._____
informal social control is that exerted by

    A. public opinion
    B. religious doctrine
    C. educational institutions
    D. statutes
    E. public health measures

12. The PRINCIPAL function of the jury in a jury trial is to decide questions of 12._____

    A. equity
    B. fact
    C. injunction
    D. contract
    E. law

13. Of the following rights of an individual, the one which usually depends on citizenship as distinguished from those given anyone living under the laws of the United States is the right to   13._____

    A. receive public assistance
    B. hold an elective office
    C. petition the government for redress of grievances
    D. receive equal protection of the laws
    E. be accorded a trial by jury

14. If the characteristics of a person were being studied by competent observers, it would be expected that their observations would differ MOST markedly with respect to their evaluation of the person's   14._____

    A. intelligence
    B. nutritional condition
    C. temperamental characteristics
    D. weight
    E. height

15. If there are evidences of dietary deficiency in families where cereals make up a major portion of the diet, the *most likely* reason for this deficiency is that   15._____

    A. cereals cause absorption of excessive quantities of water
    B. persons who concentrate their diet on cereals do not chew their food properly
    C. carbohydrates are deleterious
    D. other essential food elements are omitted
    E. children eat cereals too rapidly

16. Although malnutrition is generally associated with poverty, dietary studies of population groups in the United States reveal that   16._____

    A. malnutrition is most often due to a deficiency of nutrients found chiefly in high-cost foods
    B. there has been overemphasis of the casual relationship between poverty and malnutrition
    C. malnutrition is found among people with sufficient money to be well fed
    D. a majority of the population in all income groups is undernourished
    E. malnutrition is not a factor in the incidence of rickets

17. The organization which has as one of its primary functions the mitigation of suffering caused by famine, fire, floods, and other national calamities is the   17._____

    A. National Safety Council
    B. Salvation Army
    C. Public Administration Service
    D. American National Red Cross
    E. American Legion

18. The MAIN difference between public welfare and private social agencies is that in public agencies,

    A. case records are open to the public
    B. the granting of assistance cannot be sufficiently flexible to meet the varying needs of individual recipients
    C. only financial assistance may be provided
    D. all policies and procedures must be based upon statutory authorizations
    E. economical and efficient administration are stressed because their funds are obtained through public taxation

18.____

19. A recipient of relief who is in need of the services of an attorney but is unable to pay the customary fees, should *generally* be referred to the

    A. Small Claims Court
    B. Domestic Relations Court
    C. County Lawyers Association
    D. City Law Department
    E. Legal Aid Society

19.____

20. An injured workman should file his claim for workmen's compensation with the

    A. State Labor Relations Board
    B. Division of Placement and Unemployment Insurance
    C. State Industrial Commission
    D. Workmen's Compensation Board
    E. State Insurance Board

20.____

21. The type of insurance found MOST frequently among families such as those assisted by the Department of Social Services is

    A. accident   B. straight life
    C. endowment   D. industrial
    E. personal liability

21.____

22. Of the following items in the standard budget of the Department of Social Services, the one for which actual expenditures would be MOST constant throughout the year is

    A. fuel   B. housing
    C. medical care   D. clothing
    E. household replacements

22.____

23. The MOST frequent cause of "broken homes" is attributed to the

    A. temperamental incompatibilities of parents and in-laws
    B. extension of the system of children's courts
    C. psychopathic irresponsibility of the parents
    D. institutionalization of one of the spouses
    E. death of one or both spouses

23.____

24. In rearing children, the problems of the widower are usually greater than those of the widow, largely because of the   24._____

    A.   tendency of widowers to impose excessively rigid moral standards
    B.   increased economic hardship
    C.   added difficulty of maintaining a desirable home
    D.   possibility that a stepmother will be added to the household
    E.   prevalent masculine prejudice against pursuits which are inherently feminine

25. Foster–home placement of children is often advocated in preference to institutionaliza-tion *primarily* because   25._____

    A.   the law does not provide for local supervision of children's institutions
    B.   institutions furnish a more expensive type of care
    C.   the number of institutions is insufficient compared to the number of children need-ing care
    D.   children are not well treated in institutions
    E.   foster homes provide a more normal environment for children

———

KEY (CORRECT ANSWERS)

1.	E	11.	A
2.	E	12.	B
3.	B	13.	B
4.	B	14.	C
5.	C	15.	D
6.	C	16.	C
7.	D	17.	D
8.	D	18.	D
9.	C	19.	E
10.	E	20.	D

21.	D
22.	B
23.	E
24.	C
25.	E

———

TEST 2

DIRECTIONS: Each question or incomplete statement is followed by several suggested answers or completions. Select the one that BEST answers the question or completes the statement. *PRINT THE LETTER OF THE CORRECT ANSWER IN THE SPACE AT THE RIGHT.*

1. Of the following, the category MOST likely to yield the greatest reduction in cost to the taxpayer under improved employment conditions is

    A.   home relief, including aid to the homeless
    B.   aid to the blind
    C.   aid to dependent children
    D.   old–age assistance

1.____

2. One of the MOST common characteristics of the chronic alcoholic is

    A.   low intelligence level   B.   wanderlust
    C.   psychosis   D.   egocentricity

2.____

3. Of the following factors leading toward the cure of the alcoholic, the MOST important is thought to be

    A.   removal of all alcohol from the immediate environment
    B.   development of a sense of personal adequacy
    C.   social disapproval of drinking
    D.   segregation from former companions

3.____

4. The Federal Housing Administration is the agency which

    A.   insures mortgages made by lending institutions for new construction or remodeling of old construction
    B.   provides federal aid for state and local government for slum clearance and housing for very low income families
    C.   subsidizes the building industry through direct grants
    D.   provides for the construction of low-cost housing projects owned and operated by the federal government

4.____

5. In comparing the advantages of foster home over institutional placement, it is generally agreed that institutional care is LEAST advisable for children

    A.   who cannot sustain the intimacy of foster family living because of their experiences with their own parents
    B.   who are socially well-adjusted or have had considerable experience in living with a family
    C.   who have need for special facilities for observation, diagnosis, and treatment
    D.   whose natural parents find it difficult to accept the idea of foster home placement because of its close resemblance to adoption

5.____

6. The school can play a vital part in detecting the child who displays overt symptomatic   6.____
   behavior indicative of social maladjustment CHIEFLY because the teacher has the
   opportunity to

   A. assume a pseudo-parental role in regard to discipline and punishment, thereby
      limiting the extent of the maladjusted child's anti-social behavior
   B. observe how the child relates to the group and what reactions are stimulated in him
      by his peer relationships
   C. determine whether the adjustment difficulties displayed by the child were brought
      on by the teacher herself or by the other students
   D. help the child's parents to resolve the difficulties in adjustment which are indicated
      by the child's reactions to the social pressures exerted by his peers

7. In treating juvenile delinquents, it has been found that there are some who make better   7.____
   social adjustment through group treatment than through an individual casework
   approach.
   In selecting delinquent boys for group treatment, the one of the following which is the
   MOST important consideration is that

   A. the boys to be treated in one group be friends or from the same community
   B. only boys who consent to group treatment be included in the group
   C. the ages of the boys included in the group vary as much as possible
   D. only boys who have not reacted to an individual casework approach be included in
      the group

8. Multi-problem families are generally characterized by various functional indicators.   8.____
   Of the following, the family which is *most likely* to be a multi-problem family is one
   which has

   A. unemployed adult family members
   B. parents with diagnosed character disorders
   C. children and parents with a series of difficulties in the community
   D. poor housekeeping standards

9. Multi-problem families generally have a complex history of intervention by a variety of   9.____
   social agencies.
   Of the following phases involved in planning for their treatment, the one which is MOST
   important to consider FIRST is the

   A. joint decision to limit any help to be given
   B. analysis of facts and definition of the problems involved
   C. determination of treatment priorities
   D. study of available community resources

10. The development of good public relations in the area for which the supervisor is respon-   10.____
    sible should be considered by the supervisor as

    A. not his responsibility as he is primarily responsible for his workers' services
    B. dependent upon him as he is in the best position to interpret the department to the
       community
    C. not important to the adequate functioning of the department
    D. a part of his method of carrying out his job responsibility as what his workers do
       affects the community

11. Of the following, the LEAST accurate statement concerning the relationship of public and   11.____
    private social agencies is that

    A. both have an important and necessary function to perform
    B. they are not to be considered as competing or rival agencies
    C. they are cooperating agencies
    D. their work is based on fundamentally different social work concepts

12. Of the following, the LEAST accurate statement concerning the worker-client relation-   12.____
    ship is that the worker should have the ability to

    A. express warmth of feeling in appropriate ways as a basis for a professional rela-
       tionship which creates confidence
    B. feel appropriately in the relationship without losing the ability to see the situation in
       the perspective necessary to help the people immersed in it
    C. identify himself with the client so that the worker's personality does not influence
       the client
    D. use keen observation and perceive what is significant with a new range of appreci-
       ation of the meaning of the situation to the client

13. Of the following, the MOST fundamental psychological concept underlying case work in   13.____
    the public assistance field is that

    A. eligibility for public assistance should be reviewed from time to time
    B. workers should be aware of the prevalence of psychological disabilities among
       members of families on public assistance
    C. workers should realize the necessity of carrying out the policies laid down by the
       state office in order that state aid may be received
    D. in the process of receiving assistance, recipients should not be deprived of their
       normal status of self-direction

14. Of the following, the MOST comprehensive as well as the MOST accurate statement   14.____
    concerning the professional attitude of the social worker is that he should

    A. have a real concern for, and an intelligent interest in, the welfare of the client
    B. recognize that the client's feelings rather than the realities of his needs are of major
       importance to the client
    C. put at the client's service the worker's knowledge and sincere interest in him
    D. use his insight and understanding to make sound decisions about the client

15. The one of the following reasons for refusing a job which is LEAST acceptable, from the   15._____
viewpoint of maintaining a client's continued rights to unemployment insurance benefits,
is that

    A.   acceptance of the job would interfere with the client's joining or retaining member-
ship in a labor union
    B.   there is a strike, lockout, or other industrial controversy in the establishment where
employment is offered
    C.   the distance from the place of employment to his home is greater than seems justi-
fied to the client
    D.   the wages offered are lower than the prevailing wages in that locality

16. Experience pragmatically suggests that dislocation from cultural roots and customs   16._____
makes for tension, insecurity, and anxiety. This holds for the child as well as the adoles-
cent, for the new immigrant as well as the second-generation citizen.
Of the following, the MOST important implication of the above statement for a social
worker in any setting is that

    A.   anxiety, distress, and incapacity are always personal and can be understood best
only through an understanding of the child's present cultural environment
    B.   in order to resolve the conflicts caused by the displacement of a child from a home
with one cultural background to one with another, it is essential that the child fully
replace his old culture with the new one
    C.   no treatment goal can be envisaged for a dislocated child which does not involve a
value judgment which is itself culturally determined
    D.   anxiety and distress result from a child's reaction to culturally oriented treatment
goals

17. Accepting the fact that mentally gifted children represent superior heredity, the United   17._____
States faces an important eugenic problem CHIEFLY because

    A.   unless these mentally gifted children mature and reproduce more rapidly than the
less intelligent children, the nation is heading for a lowering of the average intelligence of its people
    B.   although the mentally gifted child always excels scholastically, he generally has
less physical stamina than the normal child and tends to lower the nation's population physically
    C.   the mentally subnormal are increasing more rapidly than the mentally gifted in
America, thus affecting the overall level of achievement of the gifted child
    D.   unless the mental level of the general population is raised to that of the gifted child,
the mentally gifted will eventually usurp the reigns of government and dominate the
mentally weaker

18. The form of psychiatric treatment which requires the LEAST amount of participation on   18._____
the part of the patient is

    A.   psychoanalysis   B.   psychotherapy
    C.   shock therapy   D.   non-directive therapy

19. Tests administered by psychologists for the PRIMARY purpose of measuring intelligence are known as _____ tests.

    A. projective
    C. psychometric
    B. validating
    D. apperception

19.____

20. In recent years, there have been some significant changes in the treatment of patients in state psychiatric hospitals. These changes are PRIMARILY caused by the use of

    A. electric shock therapy
    B. tranquilizing drugs
    C. steroids
    D. the open-ward policy

20.____

21. The psychological test which makes use of a set of twenty pictures, each depicting a dramatic scene, is known as the

    A. Goodenough Test
    B. Thematic Apperception Test
    C. Minnesota Multiphasic Personality Inventory
    D. Healy Picture Completion Test

21.____

22. One of the MOST effective ways in which experimental psychologists have been able to study the effects on personality of heredity and environment has been through the study of

    A. primitive cultures
    C. mental defectives
    B. identical twins
    D. newborn infants

22.____

23. In hospitals with psychiatric divisions, the psychiatric function is PREDOMINANTLY that of

    A. the training of personnel in all psychiatric disciplines
    B. protection of the community against potentially dangerous psychiatric patients
    C. research and study of psychiatric patients so that new knowledge and information can be made generally available
    D. short-term hospitalization designed to determine diagnosis and recommendations for treatment

23.____

24. Predictions of human behavior on the basis of past behavior frequently are INACCURATE because

    A. basic patterns of human behavior are in a continual state of flux
    B. human behavior is not susceptible to explanation of a scientific nature
    C. the underlying psychological mechanisms of behavior are not completely understood
    D. quantitative techniques for the measurement of stimuli and responses are unavailable

24.____

25. Socio-cultural factors are being re-evaluated in casework practice as they influence both   25.____
the worker and the client in their participation in the casework process.
Of the following factors, the one which is currently being studied MOST widely is the

    A.   social class of worker and client and its significance in casework
    B.   difference in native intelligence which can be ascribed to racial origin of an individual
    C.   cultural values affecting the areas in which an individual functions
    D.   necessity in casework treatment of the client's membership in an organized religious group

---

KEY (CORRECT ANSWERS)

1.	A		11.	D
2.	D		12.	C
3.	B		13.	D
4.	A		14.	C
5.	B		15.	C
6.	B		16.	C
7.	B		17.	A
8.	C		18.	C
9.	B		19.	C
10.	D		20.	B

21.	B
22.	B
23.	D
24.	C
25.	C

EXAMINATION SECTION
TEST 1

DIRECTIONS: Each question or incomplete statement is followed by several suggested
answers or completions. Select the one that BEST answers the question or
completes the statement. *PRINT THE LETTER OF THE CORRECT ANSWER
IN THE SPACE AT THE RIGHT.*

1.   Deviant behavior is a sociological term used to describe behavior which is not in accord   1.____
with generally accepted standards. This may include juvenile delinquency, adult criminal-
ity, mental or physical illness.
Comparison of normal with deviant behavior is useful to social workers because it

   A.   makes it possible to establish watertight behavioral descriptions
   B.   provides evidence of differential social behavior which distinguishes deviant from
normal behavior
   C.   indicates that deviant behavior is of no concern to social workers
   D.   provides no evidence that social role is a determinant of behavior

2.   Alcoholism may affect an individual client's ability to function as a spouse, parent, worker,   2.____
and citizen.
A social worker's MAIN responsibility to a client with a history of alcoholism is to

   A.   interpret to the client the causes of alcoholism as a disease syndrome
   B.   work with the alcoholic's family to accept him as he is and stop trying to reform him
   C.   encourage the family of the alcoholic to accept casework treatment
   D.   determine the origins of his particular drinking problem, establish a diagnosis, and
work out a treatment plan for him

3.   There is a trend to regard narcotic addiction as a form of illness for which the current   3.____
methods of intervention have not been effective.
Research on the combination of social, psychological, and physical causes of addiction would indicate that social workers should

   A.   oppose hospitalization of addicts in institutions
   B.   encourage the addict to live normally at home
   C.   recognize that there is no successful treatment for addiction and act accordingly
   D.   use the existing community facilities differentially for each addict

4.   A study of social relationships among delinquent and non-delinquent youth has shown   4.____
that

   A.   delinquent youth generally conceal their true feelings and maintain furtive social
contacts
   B.   delinquents are more impulsive and vivacious than law-abiding boys
   C.   non-delinquent youths diminish their active social relationships in order to subli-
mate any anti-social impulses
   D.   delinquent and non-delinquent youths exhibit similar characteristics of impulsive-
ness and vivaciousness

5. The one of the following which is the CHIEF danger of interpreting the delinquent behav-   5.____
ior of a child in terms of morality *alone* when attempting to get at its causes is that

    A.   this tends to overlook the likelihood that the causes of the child's actions are more
than a negation of morality and involve varied symptoms of disturbance

    B.   a child's moral outlook toward life and society is largely colored by that of his par-
ents, thus encouraging parent-child conflict

    C.   too careful a consideration of the moral aspects of the offense and of the child's
needs may often negate the demands of justice in a case

    D.   standards of morality may be of no concern to the delinquent and he may not real-
ize the seriousness of his offenses

6. Experts in the field of personnel administration are generally agreed that an employee   6.____
should not be under the immediate supervision of more than one supervisor. A certain
worker, because of an emergency situation, divides his time equally between two limited
caseloads on a prearranged time schedule. Each unit has a different supervisor, and the
worker performs substantially the same duties in each caseload.
The above statement is pertinent in this situation CHIEFLY because

    A.   each supervisor, feeling that the cases in her unit should have priority, may
demand too much of the worker's time

    B.   the two supervisors may have different standards of work performance and may
prefer different methods of doing the work

    C.   the worker works part-time on each caseload and may not have full knowledge or
control of the situation in either caseload

    D.   the task of evaluating the worker's services will be doubled, with two supervisors
instead of one having to rate his work

7. Experts in modern personnel management generally agree that employees on all job lev-   7.____
els should be permitted to offer suggestions for improving work methods.
Of the following, the CHIEF limitation of such suggestions is that they may, at times,

    A.   be offered primarily for financial reward and not show genuine interest in improve-
ment of work methods

    B.   be directed towards making individual jobs easier

    C.   be restricted by the employees' fear of radically changing the work methods
favored by their supervisors

    D.   show little awareness of the effects on the overall objectives and functions of the
entire agency

8. Through the supervisory process and relationship, the supervisor is trying to help work-   8.____
ers gain increased self-awareness.
Of the following statements concerning this process, the one which is MOST accurate
is:

    A.   Self-awareness is developed gradually so that worker can learn to control his own
reactions.

    B.   Worker is expected to be introspective primarily for his own enlightenment.

    C.   Supervisor is trying to help worker handle any emotional difficulties he may reveal.

    D.   Worker is expected at the onset to share and determine with the supervisor what in
his previous background makes it difficult for him to use certain ideas.

9. The one of the following statements concerning principles in the learning process which   9.____
    is LEAST accurate is:

    A. Some degree of regression on the part of the worker is usually natural in the pro-
        cess of development and this should be accepted by the supervisor.
    B. When a beginning worker shows problems, the supervisor should first handle this
        behavior as a personality difficulty.
    C. It has been found in the work training process that some degree of resistance is
        usually inevitable.
    D. The emotional content of work practice may tend to set up *blind spots* in workers.

10. Of the following, the one that represents the BEST basis for planning the content of a   10.____
    successful staff development program is the

    A. time available for meetings
    B. chief social problems of the community
    C. common needs of the staff workers as related to the situations with which they are
        dealing
    D. experimental programs conducted by other agencies

11. In planning staff development seminars, the MOST valuable topics for discussion are   11.____
    likely to be those selected from

    A. staff suggestions based on the staff's interest and needs
    B. topics recommended for consideration by professional organizations
    C. topics selected by the administration based on demonstrated limitations of staff
        skill and knowledge
    D. topics selected by the administration based on a combination of staff interest and
        objectivity evaluated staff needs

12. Staff meetings designed to promote professional staff development are MOST likely to   12.____
    achieve this goal when

    A. there is the widest participation among all staff members who attend the meetings
    B. participation by the most skilled and experienced staff members is predominant
    C. participation by selected staff members is planned before the meeting sessions
    D. supervisory personnel take major responsibility for participation

13. Assume that you are the leader of a conference attended by representatives of various   13.____
    city and private agencies. After the conference has been underway for a considerable
    time, you realize that the representative of one of these agencies has said nothing.
    It would generally be BEST for you to

    A. ask him if he would like to say anything
    B. ask the group a pertinent question that he would probably be best able to answer
    C. make no special effort to include him in the conversation
    D. address the next question you planned to ask to him directly

14. A member of a decision-making conference generally makes his BEST contribution to   14.____
    the conference when he

    A. compromises on his own point of view and accepts most of the points of other con-
        ference members
    B. persuades the conference to accept all or most of his points

C. persuades the conference to accept his major proposals but will yield on the minor ones
D. succeeds in integrating his ideas with the ideas of the other conference members

15. Of the following, the LEAST accurate statement concerning the compilation and use of statistics in administration is:　　15.____

A. Interpretation of statistics is as necessary as their compilation.
B. Statistical records of expenditures and services are one of the bases for budget preparation.
C. Statistics on the quality of services rendered to the community will clearly delineate the human values achieved.
D. The results achieved from collecting and compiling statistics must be in keeping with the cost and effort required.

16. An important administrative problem is how precisely to define the limits on authority that is delegated to subordinate supervisors.　　16.____
Such definition of limits of authority SHOULD be

A. as precise as possible and practicable in all areas
B. as precise as possible and practicable in all areas of function,but should allow con- siderable flexibility in the area of personnel management
C. as precise as possible and practicable in the area of personnel management, but should allow considerable flexibility in the areas of function
D. in general terms so as to allow considerable flexibility both in the areas of function and in the areas of personnel management

17. The LEAST important of the following reasons why a particular activity should be assigned to a unit which performs activities dissimilar to it is that　　17.____

A. close coordination is needed between the particular activity and other activities performed by the unit
B. it will enhance the reputation and prestige of the unit supervisor
C. the unit makes frequent use of the results of this particular activity
D. the unit supervisor has a sound knowledge and understanding of the particular activity

18. The MOST important of the following reasons why the average resident of a deteriorated slum neighborhood resists relocation to an area in the suburbs with better physical accommodations is that he　　18.____

A. does not recognize as undesirable the characteristics which are responsible for deterioration of the neighborhood
B. has some expectation of neighborly assistance in his old home in times of stress and adversity
C. hopes for better days when he may be able to become a figure of some importance and envy in the old neighborhood
D. is attuned to the noise of the city and fears the quiet of the suburb

19. From a psychological and sociological point of view, the MOST important of the following   19.____
    dangers to the persons living in an economically depressed area in which the only step
    taken by governmental and private social agencies to assist these persons is the grant-
    ing of a dole is that

    A. industry will be reluctant to expand its operations in that area
    B. the dole will encourage additional non-producers to enter the area
    C. the residents of the area will probably have to find their own solution to their prob-
        lems
    D. their permanent dependency will be fostered

20. The term *real wages* is GENERALLY used by economists to mean the   20.____

    A. amount of take-home pay left after taxes, social security, and other such deduc-
        tions have been made by the employer
    B. average wage actually earned during a calendar or fiscal year
    C. family income expressed on a per capita basis
    D. wages expressed in terms of its buyer power

21. It has, at times, been suggested that an effective way to eradicate juvenile delinquency   21.____
    would be to arrest and punish the parents for the criminal actions of their delinquent chil-
    dren.
    The one of the following which is the CHIEF defect of this proposal is that

    A. it fails to get at the cause of the delinquent act and tends to further weaken dis-
        turbed parent-child relationships
    B. since the criminally inclined child has apparently demonstrated little love or affec-
        tion for his parent, the child will be unlikely to amend his behavior in order to avoid
        hurting his parent
    C. the child who commits anti-social acts does so in many cases in order to hurt his
        parents so that this proposal would not only increase the parents' sorrow, but
        would also serve as an incentive to more delinquency by the child
    D. the punishment should be limited to the person who commits the illegal action
        rather than to those who are most interested in his welfare

22. Surveys which have compared the relative stability of marriages between white persons   22.____
    with marriages between non-white persons in this country have shown that, among
    Blacks, there is

    A. a significantly higher percentage of spouses absent from the household than
        among whites
    B. a significantly higher percentage of spouses absent from the household than
        among whites living in the South, but the opposite is true in the Northeast
    C. a significantly lower percentage of spouses absent from the household than
        among whites
    D. no significant difference in the percentage of spouses absent from the household
        when compared with the white population

23. A phenomenon found in the cultural and recreational patterns of European immigrant families in America is that, generally, the foreign-born adults   23._____

   A. as well as their children, tend soon to forget their old-world activities and adopt the cultural and recreational customs of America
   B. as well as their children, tend to retain and continue their old-world cultural and recreational pursuits, and find it equally difficult to adopt those of America
   C. tend soon to drop their old pursuits and adopt the cultural and recreational patterns of America while their children find it somewhat more difficult to make this change
   D. tend to retain and continue their old-world cultural and recreational pursuits while their children tend to rapidly replace these by the games and cultural patterns of America

24. Certain mores of migrant groups are strengthened under the impact of their contact with the native society while other mores are weakened.   24._____
   In the case of Puerto Ricans who have come to the city, the effect of such contact upon their traditional family structure has been a

   A. strengthening of the former maternalistic family structure
   B. strengthening of the former paternalistic family structure
   C. weakening of the former maternalistic family structure
   D. weakening of the former paternalistic family structure

25. Administrative reviews and special studies of independent experts, as reported by the Department of Health, Education and Welfare, indicate that the proportion of recipients of public assistance who receive such assistance through *wilful misrepresentation* of the facts is   25._____

   A. less than 1%   B. about 4%
   C. between 4% and 7%   D. between 7% and 10%

KEY (CORRECT ANSWERS)

1.	B	11.	D
2.	D	12.	A
3.	D	13.	B
4.	B	14.	D
5.	A	15.	C
6.	B	16.	A
7.	D	17.	B
8.	A	18.	B
9.	B	19.	D
10.	C	20.	D

21.	A
22.	A
23.	D
24.	D
25.	A

TEST 2

DIRECTIONS: Each question or incomplete statement is followed by several suggested answers or completions. Select the one that BEST answers the question or completes the statement. *PRINT THE LETTER OF THE CORRECT ANSWER IN THE SPACE AT THE RIGHT.*

1. In order to meet more adequately the public assistance needs occasioned by sudden changes in the national economy, social service agencies, in general, recommend, as a matter of preference, that

   A. each locality build up reserve funds to care for needy unemployed persons in order to avoid a breakdown of local resources such as occurred during the depression
   B. the federal government assume total responsibility for the administration of public assistance
   C. state settlement laws be strictly enforced so that unemployed workers will be encouraged to move from the emergency industry centers to their former homes
   D. a federal-state-local program of general assistance be established with need as the only eligibility requirement
   E. eligibility requirements be tightened to assure that only legitimately worthy local residents receive the available assistance

   1.____

2. The MOST practical method of maintaining income for the majority of aged persons who are no longer able to work, or for the families of those workers who are deceased, is a(n)

   A. comprehensive system of non-categorical assistance on a basis of cash payments
   B. integrated system of public assistance and extensive work relief programs
   C. co-ordinated system of providing care in institutions and foster homes
   D. system of contributory insurance in which a cash benefit is paid as a matter of right
   E. expanded system of diagnostic and treatment centers

   2.____

3. With the establishment of insurance and assistance programs under the Social Security Act, many institutional programs for the aged have tended to the greatest extent toward an increased emphasis on providing, of the following types of assistance,

   A. care for the aged by denominational groups
   B. care for children requiring institutional treatment
   C. recreational facilities for the able-bodied aged
   D. training facilities in industrial homework for the aged
   E. care for the chronically ill and infirm aged

   3.____

4. Of the following terms, the one which BEST describes the Social Security Act is

   A. enabling legislation
   B. regulatory statute
   C. appropriations act
   D. act of mandamus
   E. provisional enactment

   4.____

5. Of the following, the term which MOST accurately describes an appropriation is 5.____

    A. authority to spend
    B. itemized estimate
    C. *fund* accounting
    D. anticipated expenditure
    E. executive budget

6. When business expansion causes a demand for labor, the worker group which benefits MOST immediately is the group comprising 6.____

    A. employed workers
    B. inexperienced workers under 21 years of age
    C. experienced workers 21 to 25 years of age
    D. inexperienced older workers
    E. experienced workers over 40 years of age

7. The MOST important failure in our present system of providing social work services in local communities is the 7.____

    A. absence of adequate facilities for treating mental illness
    B. lack of coordination of available data and service in the community
    C. poor quality of the casework services provided by the public agencies
    D. limitations of the probation and parole services
    E. inadequacy of private family welfare services

8. Recent studies of the relationship between incidence of illness and the use of available treatment services among various population groups in the United States show that 8.____

    A. while lower-income families use medical services with greater frequency, total expenditures are greater among the upper-income groups
    B. although the average duration of a period of medical care increases with increasing income, the average frequency of obtaining care decreases with increasing income
    C. adequacy of medical service is inversely related to frequency of illness and size of family income
    D. families in the higher-income brackets have a heavier incidence of illness and make greater use of medical services than do those in the lower-income brackets
    E. both as to frequency and duration, the distribution of illness falls equally on all groups, but the use of medical services increases with income

9. The category of disease which most public health departments and authorities usually are NOT equipped to handle *directly* is that of 9.____

    A. chronic disease
    B. bronchial disturbances
    C. venereal disease
    D. mosquito-borne diseases
    E. incipient forms of tuberculosis

10. Recent statistical analyses of the causes of death in the United States indicate that medical science has now reached the stage where it would be preferable to increase its research toward control, among the following, PRINCIPALLY of

    A. accidents
    B. suicides
    C. communicable disease
    D. chronic disease
    E. infant mortality

10.____

11. Although the distinction between mental disease and mental deficiency is fairly definite, both these conditions USUALLY represent

    A. diseases of one part or organ of the body rather than of the whole person
    B. an inadequacy existing from birth or shortly afterwards and appearing as a simplicity of intelligence
    C. a deficiency developing later in life and characterized by distortions of attitude and belief
    D. inadequacies in meeting life situations and in conducting one's affairs
    E. somewhat transitory conditions characterized by disturbances of consciousness

11.____

12. According to studies made by reliable medical research organizations in the United States, differences among the states in proportion of physicians to population are MOST directly related to the

    A. geographic resources among the states
    B. skill of the physicians
    C. relative proportions of urban and rural people in the population of the states
    D. number of specialists in the ranks of the physicians
    E. health status of the people in the various states

12.____

13. One of the MAIN advantages of incorporating a charitable organization is that

    A. gifts or property of a corporation cannot be held in perpetuity
    B. gifts to unincorporated charitable organizations are not deductible from the taxable income
    C. incorporation gives less legal standing or *personality* than an informal partnership
    D. members of a corporation cannot be held liable for debts contracted by the organization
    E. a corporate organization cannot be sued

13.____

14. The BASIC principle underlying a social security program is that the government should provide

    A. aid to families that is not dependent on state or local participation
    B. assistance to any worthy family unable to maintain itself independently
    C. protection to individuals against some of the social risks that are inherent in an industrialized society
    D. safeguards against those factors leading to economic depression

14.____

15. The activities of state and local public welfare agencies are dependent to a large degree on the public assistance program of the federal government.
The one of the following which the federal government has NOT been successful in achieving within the local agencies is the

    A. broadening of the scope of public assistance administration
    B. expansion of the categorical programs
    C. improvement of the quality of service given to clients
    D. standardization of the administration of general assistance programs

15.____

16. Of the following statements, the one which BEST describes the federal government's position, as stated in the Social Security Act, with regard to tests of character or fitness to be administered by local or state welfare departments to prospective clients is that

    A. no tests of character are required but they are not specifically prohibited
    B. if tests of character are used, they must be uniform throughout the state
    C. tests of character are contrary to the philosophy of the federal government and are to be considered illegal
    D. no tests of character are required, and assistance to those states that use them will be withheld

16.____

17. An increase in the size of the welfare grant may increase the cost of the welfare program not only in terms of those already on the welfare rolls, but because it may result in an increase in the number of people on the rolls.
The CHIEF reason that an increase in the size of the grant may cause an increase in the number of people on the rolls is that the increased grant may

    A. induce low-salaried wage earners to apply for assistance rather than continue at their menial jobs
    B. make eligible for assistance many people whose resources are just above the previous standard
    C. induce many people to apply for assistance who hesitated to do so because of meagerness of the previous grant
    D. make relatives less willing to contribute because the welfare grant can more adequately cover their dependents' needs

17.____

18. One of the MAIN differences between the use of casework methods by a public welfare agency and by a private welfare agency is that the public welfare agency

    A. requires that the applicant be eligible for the services it offers
    B. cannot maintain a non-judgmental attitude toward its clients because of legal requirements
    C. places less emphasis on efforts to change the behavior of its clients
    D. must be more objective in its approach to the client because public funds are involved

18.____

19. All definitions of social casework include certain major assumptions.
Of the following, the one which is NOT considered a major assumption is that

    A. the individual and society are interdependent
    B. social forces influence behavior and attitudes, affording opportunity for self-development and contribution to the world in which we live
    C. reconstruction of the total personality and reorganization of the total environment are specific goals
    D. the client is a responsible participant at every step in the solution of his problems

19.____

20. In order to provide those services to problem families which will help restore them to a self-maintaining status, it is necessary to FIRST

    A. develop specific plans to meet the individual needs of the problem family
    B. reduce the size of those caseloads composed of multi-problem families
    C. remove them from their environment and provide them with the means of overcoming their dependency
    D. identify the factors causing their dependency and creating problems for them

20.____

21. Of the following, the type of service which can provide the client with the MOST enduring help is that service which

    A. provides him with material aid and relieves the stress of his personal problems
    B. assists him to do as much as he can for himself and leaves him free to make his own decisions
    C. directs his efforts towards returning to a self-maintaining status and provides him with desirable goals
    D. gives him the feeling that the agency is interested in him as an individual and stands ready to assist him with his problems

21.____

22. Psychiatric interpretation of unconscious motivations can bring childhood conflicts into the framework of adult understanding and open the way for them to be resolved, but the interpretation must come from within the client.
This statement means MOST NEARLY that

    A. treatment is merely diagnosis in reverse
    B. explaining a client to himself will lead to the resolution of his problems
    C. the client must arrive at an understanding of his problems
    D. unresolved childhood conflicts create problems for the adult

22.____

23. A significant factor in the United States economic picture is the state of the labor market. Of the following, the MOST important development affecting the labor market has been

    A. an expansion of the national defense effort creating new plant capacity
    B. the general increase in personal income as a result of an increase in overtime pay in manufacturing industries
    C. the growth of manufacturing as a result of automation
    D. a demand for a large number of jobs resulting from new job applicants as well as from displacement of workers by automation

23.____

24. A typical characteristic of the United States population over 65 is that MOST of them

    A. are independent and capable of self-support
    B. live in their own homes but require various supportive services
    C. live in institutions for the aged
    D. require constant medical attention at home or in an institution

24.____

25. The one of the following factors which is MOST important in preventing persons 65 years of age and older from getting employment is the

    A. misconceptions by employers of skills and abilities of senior citizens
    B. lack of skill in modern industrial techniques of persons in this age group
    C. social security laws restricting employment of persons in this age group
    D. unwillingness of persons in this age group to continue supporting themselves

25.____

KEY (CORRECT ANSWERS)

1.	D		11.	D
2.	D		12.	C
3.	E		13.	D
4.	A		14.	C
5.	A		15.	D
6.	B		16.	A
7.	B		17.	B
8.	C		18.	C
9.	A		19.	C
10.	D		20.	D

21. B
22. C
23. D
24. B
25. A

———

EXAMINATION SECTION
TEST 1

DIRECTIONS: Each question or incomplete statement is followed by several suggested answers or completions. Select the one that BEST answers the question or completes the statement. *PRINT THE LETTER OF THE CORRECT ANSWER IN THE SPACE AT THE RIGHT.*

1. One day an elderly man asks you if he can apply for Social Security at the welfare office. Your response should be to   1.____

   A. tell him that it is foolish to think he can apply for Social Security at the welfare office
   B. take him back to his apartment because he is too old to be roaming the streets asking questions
   C. explain that Social Security is a federal program and direct him to the nearest Social Security office
   D. call his daughter and tell her that the family should take better care of their father

2. One of your duties is to occasionally visit clients. On one occasion, you visit Mrs. B., who needs assistance in referral of her children for day care so that she may enter a job training program. She has postponed completing the referral.
   What should you do in this situation?   2.____

   A. Tell her that if she doesn't hurry there will be no room at the day care center and the training program will be closed.
   B. Make the arrangements and tell Mrs. B. that she should do what you say.
   C. Remember that all people who ask for help are not always ready to receive it and continue to allow Mrs. B. time to complete the referral by herself.
   D. The next time Mrs. B. asks for help, see that she gets it as slowly as possible.

3. Assume that you are trying to contact a community group to offer to meet with their representative to explain a new agency policy about intake procedures.
   In order to "get your message across," you should   3.____

   A. write a short concise letter explaining why you want to meet with them and when you will be available
   B. write a short letter stating only that it is important that they contact you in order to arrange a meeting
   C. ask a secretary to help you because you do not really like to write to groups
   D. call the agency rather than write since you know someone there

4. It is necessary for you to call the director of a head start center in order to discuss a training program for teaching aides. The operator asks who you are and what you wish to discuss with the director.
   Your response should be to   4.____

   A. tell her that you would rather explain to the director and you want to speak to her immediately
   B. identify yourself, your department and the nature of your business with the director
   C. hang up and try to call again when another operator is on duty
   D. tell your supervisor that the operator at the head start center is rude and you would rather not be asked to call there again

5. Mrs. A. wants her children to go to summer camp. She has received the request forms, but does not understand all of the questions and you are asked to help her complete them. She comes to the office at the appointed time.
Of the following, the action you should take is to

    A. tell her she has taken so long that maybe the children will not go to camp
    B. see her as quickly as possible, explain the questions to her and help her in completing the forms
    C. help her, but tell her she will have to learn to read better and refer her to an evening school
    D. fill out the forms for her by yourself

5.____

6. Mrs. B. needs a referral to the cancer clinic. You contact the clinic and make arrangements for her visit. You go to her home to inform her about the time because she has no phone. She thanks you for your help and then offers you a piece of jewelry that appears to be rather expensive. Of the following, the action you should take is to

    A. take the gift because you don't want to hurt her feelings
    B. tell her that she is foolish and should spend her money on herself
    C. explain to her that you are pleased with her thoughtfulness, but you are unable to accept the gift
    D. refuse the gift and get someone else to make referrals in the future because she is trying to pay you for your help

6.____

7. Mrs. C., a seemingly healthy, intelligent woman whose husband is disabled, and who works part time, asks for help in getting homemaker services.
Of the following, the action you should take is to

    A. give Mrs. C. the necessary information and help her get the services
    B. tell Mrs. C. that you do not feel she needs these services since her husband is capable of helping
    C. make note of her request since you do not feel it is urgent
    D. refer her to a caseworker since she obviously needs help in defining her role as a woman

7.____

8. When you are interviewing clients, it is important to notice and record how they say what they say - angrily, nervously, or with "body English" - because these signs may

    A. tell you that the client's words are the opposite of what the client feels and you may need to dig to find out what those feelings are
    B. be the prelude to violent behavior which no aide is prepared to handle
    C. show that the client does not really deserve serious consideration
    D. be important later should you be asked to defend what you did for the client

8.____

9. You are recording a visit you have made with a client who was angry and abusive to you during the interview. At one point you lost your temper and said some things that you immediately regretted. You are embarrassed to record that you lost your temper. However, it would be desirable to record this MAINLY because

    A. you would feel guilty if you did not record it
    B. your supervisor might hear about it from the client, so it would be better to have it written down from your point of view
    C. your supervisor can use the information to help you to improve your skills
    D. it is agency policy to write down everything

9.____

10. Through one of your clients you learn that a day care program's hours have been   10.____
extended. You confirm this information with the day care center.
It is then MOST important for you to

    A. make a note of this fact, since it will mean you have to change your schedule in
working with the client
    B. add this information to your personal resource file so that you can refer other clients to the day care program
    C. inform your supervisor of the new information so that it can be added to the central
resource file
    D. ignore the information, since your client does not need to have her child in day care
for any extra hours

11. You are sent to a meeting of day-care parents to explain the programs of your agency.   11.____
One of the parents becomes very angry, saying that welfare departments treat people
like animals.
You should remain as calm as possible and say to the parent that

    A. he is right, but you have no control over what your agency does
    B. he is disrupting the meeting and you have come to explain a program, not to listen
to complaints
    C. you understand his feelings and that sometimes clients do not get the services
they wish as quickly as possible; however, you will do whatever you can to assist
him
    D. he should call your supervisor tomorrow and make an appointment to discuss his
feelings

12. Assume that you receive a telephone call from a very angry father. His daughter took   12.____
money from his wallet, and he wants the caseworker to control the daughter. He yells,
screams and swears at you.
What is the BEST way for you to respond?

    A. Hang up because you are not responsible for his daughter's actions. He shouldn't
scream and swear at you.
    B. Remember to be courteous and polite at all times, never losing your temper
despite the circumstances. Listen to him and assure him that the caseworker will
receive his message.
    C. Transfer the call to the supervisor because you are concerned about the father's
unreasonableness and do not want the responsibility of dealing with him.
    D. Tell him that behavior such as he is demonstrating is the reason his daughter
steals from him.

13. Mrs. D.'s son, aged 12, has been getting into difficulty in the neighborhood. At a commu-   13.____
nity meeting, she asks your help in finding worthwhile activities for him.
It is *appropriate* for you to respond to her because

    A. you should have knowledge of the social services available in the neighborhood
and the activities they offer
    B. you have known Mrs. D. and her family for several years and know how much trouble she has had with her son
    C. it is your job to do what the caseworker assigns to you without question
    D. you are concerned about impressing Mrs. D. with your knowledge

14. Several clients live in your neighborhood. They know that you work for the human resources administration. One day one of them tells you that there is a rumor that another client is pregnant and asks if this is true. You know from a past discussion with the caseworker that this client is pregnant.
The BEST answer for you to give would be to

    14._____

    A. tell her it is none of her business and if she wants to know, she should ask the caseworker
    B. ask her who told her that this client is pregnant
    C. explain that anything told to the agency is held in confidence and will not be shared with anyone else
    D. tell her you don't know, but will ask when you get back to the office and let her know later

15. The area senior-citizens group asks for an agency representative to discuss old-age assistance and new SSI regulations. Your supervisor asks you to attend this meeting; however, you do not wish to go because you really do not feel that you work well with older people. In fact, you don't like them very much.
What should be your response?

    15._____

    A. Tell the supervisor that you cannot go because you have an appointment with the doctor that day
    B. Get another worker to go for you and assume his task while he is gone
    C. Explain to your supervisor what problems you have in working with old-age clients
    D. Go, because you should do the tasks that are assigned to you according to your job description

16. At a center where you are distributing literature about agency programs, a citizen comes up to you and begins to complain loudly about agency programs.
What should be your response?

    16._____

    A. Call the police and have the complainer removed from the center
    B. Tell him that you do not make policy; suggest that he go to the office and complain
    C. Remain as calm as possible and ask that he discuss the complaints with you calmly. If necessary, make an appointment with him
    D. Yell at him since this seems to be the way he relates to agency people

17. A community group is having a training program. You are sent to explain agency policy and answer questions. Providing this type of contact between the agency and community groups is *proper* because

    17._____

    A. you like people and are a good public speaker
    B. it is the responsibility of the agency to cooperate with community groups in order to help the public to be well informed about agency policy
    C. you were once in the same training program and understand the kind of people who are being trained
    D. once in a while everyone should have the opportunity to speak to a community group

18. While you are assisting in the intake area, a young man who is applying is cooperative   18.____
but begins to ask you personal questions: your age, where you live, whether you have
children and other similar questions.
You are disturbed by these questions, so you should

    A. tell him that agency policy does not allow you to answer personal questions and
send him to another intake worker
    B. tell him it is your responsibility to ask questions, not his
    C. tell your supervisor that you do not want to work in intake because clients can get
too nosy and you get nervous
    D. avoid answering personal questions and try to get him to return to the purpose of
the interview

19. You are assigned to the reception area for the day. A mother arrives in the office with   19.____
three small children. In a rage, she says that she does not have enough money to feed
the children and demands that you find a home for them.
The BEST action for you to take should be to

    A. call a security officer and have him remove her and the children from the office
    B. attempt to calm her down by listening to her, attend to the children's needs and call
for a supervisor
    C. take the children from her and ask her to leave at once
    D. call the supervisor and security because it is their job to take care of abusive cli-
ents

20. Assume that you are interviewing a young unwed mother who has recently arrived in the   20.____
city from Alabama. She is a likable girl and is very cooperative. However, it is difficult to
understand the meaning of her conversation, due to her accent and different use of
words.
You would like to establish a good relationship with her, so you should FIRST

    A. suggest that she go to evening school so that she can learn to speak like other
people in the city
    B. tell her that you don't understand her sometimes and you would appreciate it if she
would explain what she means
    C. take another worker with you on visits to help you in the interview
    D. try to find a worker in the agency who has a similar background and have the case
handled by the worker

21. A man being interviewed is entitled to Medicaid, but he refuses to sign up for it because   21.____
he says he cannot accept any form of welfare. Of the following, the BEST course of
action for an aide to take FIRST is to

    A. try to discover the reason for his feeling this way
    B. tell him that he should be glad financial help is available
    C. explain that others cannot help him if he will not help himself
    D. suggest that he speak to someone who is already on Medicaid

22. Of the following, the outcome of an interview by an aide depends MOST heavily on the   22.____

    A. personality of the interviewee
    B. personality of the aide

C. subject matter of the questions asked
D. interaction between aide and interviewee

23. Some patients being interviewed are primarily interested in making a favorable impression. The aide should be aware of the fact that such patients are more likely than other patients to 23.____

A. try to anticipate the answers the interviewer is looking for
B. answer all questions openly and frankly
C. try to assume the role of interviewer
D. be anxious to get the interview over as quickly as possible

24. The type of interview which an aide usually conducts is substantially different from most interviewing situations in all of the following aspects EXCEPT the 24.____

A. setting   B. kinds of clients
C. techniques employed   D. kinds of problems

25. During an interview, an aide uses a "leading question." This type of question is so-called because it generally 25.____

A. starts a series of questions about one topic
B. suggests the answer which the aide wants
C. forms the basis for a following "trick" question
D. sets, at the beginning, the tone of the interview

KEY(CORRECT ANSWERS)

1. C		11. C	
2. C		12. B	
3. A		13. A	
4. B		14. C	
5. B		15. C	
6. C		16. C	
7. A		17. B	
8. A		18. D	
9. C		19. B	
10. C		20. B	

21. A
22. D
23. A
24. C
25. B

TEST 2

DIRECTIONS : Each question or incomplete statement is followed by several suggested answers or completions. Select the one that BEST answers the question or completes the statement. *PRINT THE LETTER OF THE CORRECT ANSWER IN THE SPACE AT THE RIGHT.*

1. Miss Lally is an old-age assistance recipient. Her health is not good and it is important that she have three good meals each day. She follows these instructions except on Friday she refuses to eat meat because of her religious beliefs. She will not even substitute fish.
   You are very concerned about this, so you should

   1.____

   A. tell your supervisor so that she will go to see Miss Lally and make her eat nourishing meals on Friday
   B. call her doctor and tell him so that he will see her and explain to her that fasting is not good for her health
   C. attempt to understand her value system and accept that it is possible that she is acting in good faith with her own values even though they may be harmful to her health
   D. explain to her how important it is that she eat meat each day in order to be in good health and enjoy the remaining years of her life

2. Theodore is a junkie. Every cent he can get his hands on legally or illegally is used to supply his habit. You are angry because the junkie is destroying himself and his family. You feel that the courts should punish him for his illegal acts.
   Of the following, the BEST action for you to take is to

   2.____

   A. suggest to your supervisor that the income maintenance center reduce the family grant, taking out his portion
   B. help his wife to find another apartment for her and the children away from him
   C. call the local police to find out why they are doing nothing about this man's activities in the community
   D. reconsider your ideas about punishment, remembering that punishment *alone* will not help the man to change his behavior

3. You are regularly assigned to taking Sarah Jones and her young son to the clinic. She is a very warm, friendly woman and your relationship with her is good. However, she invited you to come for dinner on Sunday and to go to a school play with her. You would like to accept the invitations because you need weekend activities and you like her. What should be your PRIMARY consideration in coming to a decision?

   3.____

   A. You need friends just as she does, so you should accept the invitations
   B. You are a worker and should not be seen with a client in public places
   C. Decide whether accepting the invitation will help to meet agency needs or will hamper the relationship you are expected to establish
   D. Tell her "no" because it is not a good policy to be on such friendly terms with clients

4. Martha's husband has been arrested in a drug raid and she is extremely anxious. Your supervisor asks that you visit her to determine ways in which the agency may help her. You visit and find her weeping; the house and the children have obviously been neglected.
The BEST thing for you to do is to

    4.____

    A.   tell her to stop crying and help her to clean the apartment and the children
    B.   remind her that her husband has been warned and now has to pay for not listening
    C.   listen to her, allowing her to express her feelings of fear, loss and grief, and reassure her of your concern
    D.   listen to her but caution her that she is neglecting the home and children because of her anxiety and you may have to ask your supervisor to remove the children if she doesn't get any better

5. Mrs. Dwight's landlord is very slow in making repairs in her apartment. Each time you see her, she complains about this over and over again, calling her landlord names and threatening to report him to the city. She complains to any agency person she meets. Realizing that these complaints are not getting any action, you should

    5.____

    A.   avoid meeting with her because she is annoying
    B.   suggest that she see a doctor because she is irrational and should get some help
    C.   ask her what she would like to do about the problem and assist her in carrying out her plans
    D.   ask the supervisor to see her because you do not have the skills to help her

6. In the day-to-day operations of the human resources administration, which of the following would you consider to be the PRIMARY function of the agency?

    6.____

    A.   Getting work done to meet city and federal deadlines
    B.   Being sure that all of the clients who come to the agency are seen before closing time
    C.   Delivering services to those persons who are eligible for assistance
    D.   Making sure everyone gets his check on time

7. During the course of an interview you find it is necessary to arrange a special appointment for the client to return for a further interview. After checking your calendar, you tell the client the date she is to come back. The client, however, says she cannot see you on that date because she is to attend a rally at a community center in her neighborhood.
Of the following, your BEST action should be to

    7.____

    A.   let her know that any other day is an inconvenience to you and remind her that the appointment is for her benefit
    B.   forget about the special appointment and try to get along with the information you have
    C.   explain to her the need for the appointment and ask when she can meet with you
    D.   tell her that since the community center is not city-operated, she must keep her appointment with you

8. In working with community groups, it is important that you be able to define what a community is.
Of the following definitions, which is the *most appropriate*?
A community

    8.____

    A.   consists of a group of people living fairly close together in a more or less compact territory, who come together in their chief concerns
    B.   is a particular section of a city designated on a census tract
    C.   is that portion of a city which constitutes an election district
    D.   is a section of a city or town in which a particular ethnic group conducts its social, business and religious life

9.   The agency has implemented a new policy regarding the intake procedure. You wish to explain and discuss this policy with as many community groups as possible. You make an initial contact by mail.   9._____
In order to get your message across well, your letter should be

    A.   short and as concise as possible explaining why you want to meet with them, and offer several possible times that you will be available
    B.   short, explaining only that it is important that the groups contact you in order to arrange a meeting
    C.   drafted by the center's secretary and sent to the usual groups
    D.   put in the usual announcement form in the center's newsletter

10.   A group of young welfare mothers want to form an organization that will provide baby-sitting services for mothers of children who are too young to enroll in a day care center.   10._____
What should be your answer to them?

    A.   Tell them to try to get the center to change its policy to include young children
    B.   Arrange the time to meet with them to offer as much advice and support as possible, since most communities do need this service
    C.   Suggest that it may be better that they spend their time taking care of their own children
    D.   Ask a social worker to survey the community to determine if such a service is really needed at this time

11.   New regulations have removed the disabled, blind and old age assistance cases from the public assistance caseload. Assistance in these categories is given directly by the federal government. A former client has not received his check. The chairman of the senior citizens committee calls and angrily demands that your agency do something in this man's behalf.   11._____
In response you should

    A.   answer politely, explaining that your agency is not concerned about OAA clients
    B.   arrange to meet with him in order to discuss the new policy
    C.   refer him to the Social Security office covering the area where the client lives
    D.   ask that he call again when he is calmer so that you may discuss this matter with him

12.   A high school student from the community comes to see you about a homework assignment to write a report on your center.   12._____
The BEST way to help him is to

    A.   refer him to a social worker who has daily contact with clients in their homes
    B.   contact the boy's teacher and find out why you were not warned of his coming
    C.   explain your center's program and answer as many of his questions as you can
    D.   give him literature about the welfare system in the city and state

13. Assume that the women's group of the Community Baptist Church has invited you to a Sunday afternoon service to celebrate the tenth anniversary of the pastor. The agency's relationship with the women is good in that they often offer their homes as emergency homes for adult clients. What should you do about the invitation?

    A. Do not attend but send them a note congratulating the pastor and explaining that agency personnel do not work on Sundays
    B. Ask a social worker who lives close to the church to go
    C. Accept the invitation if at all possible, attend the service and whatever social hour they may have afterwards
    D. Ignore the invitation since this function has little relationship to your job

13.____

14. Suppose that a person you are interviewing becomes angry at some of the questions you have asked, calls you meddlesome and nosy, and states that she will not answer those questions.
Of the following, which is the BEST action for you to take?

    A. Explain the reasons the questions are asked and the importance of the answers
    B. Inform the interviewee that you are only doing your job and advise her that she should answer your questions or leave your office
    C. Report to your supervisor what the interviewee called you and refuse to continue the interview
    D. End the interview and tell the interviewee she will not be serviced by your department

14.____

15. Suppose that during the course of an interview the interviewee demands in a very rude way that she be permitted to talk to your supervisor or someone in charge.
Which of the following is probably the BEST way to handle this situation?

    A. Inform your supervisor of the demand and ask her to speak to the interviewee
    B. Pay no attention to the demands of the interviewee and continue the interview
    C. Report to your supervisor and tell her to get another interviewer for this interviewee
    D. Tell her you are the one "in charge" and that she should talk to you

15.____

16. Suppose that a worker asks a client to answer several required but rather personal questions about the family's health history. The client delays and seems embarrassed about giving the answers.
Of the following, the MOST reasonable response to the client is one which

    A. shows an awareness of the client's efforts to hide something
    B. demonstrates the worker's qualifications for asking such questions
    C. allows this client to be excused from answering the questions
    D. convinces the client that his uneasiness in the situation is understood

16.____

17. A representative from a planned parenthood group comes to see you to get information for a community education program.
You should

    A. check out this group to make sure it is not promoting zero population growth for minority groups
    B. develop a good relationship with him so as to provide better service to clients
    C. make sure they will not encourage unnecessary abortions
    D. refuse to see him

17.____

18. A member of a clerical training program is continually late to classes. He explains to you that he has a hard time getting up and asks that you report him on time because he needs to train for a job.
What should your response be?

   A. Tell him that you get there on time and so should he
   B. Tell him that you do not lie for anyone
   C. Explain that it is your duty to keep accurate records and refer him to a counselor
   D. Tell him that you will cooperate with him but he has to try to do better

18.____

19. In a community meeting to explain a new agency policy, you find that the audience has no questions about the policy or your explanations.
What would be the *most appropriate* response to the silence?

   A. Leave right away before they think of questions
   B. Thank the audience for their attention and assure them that you will be available if there are any questions later
   C. Ask several members in the audience if they understand the new policy
   D. Explain that the audience could not possibly understand all of the policy and they must have questions

19.____

20. Assume that you are confronted by an angry member of the public who has not been able to obtain the information he needs from your office. You do not know the answer to his question.
The BEST thing for you to do would be to

   A. tell him to come back another time, after you have looked up the information
   B. check with your supervisor to find the correct answer
   C. tell him to ask in another office, so that you will not lose time looking for the information
   D. make up an answer to keep the man satisfied until the right answer is found

20.____

KEY (CORRECT ANSWERS)

1.	C		11.	C
2.	D		12.	C
3.	C		13.	C
4.	C		14.	A
5.	C		15.	A
6.	C		16.	D
7.	C		17.	B
8.	A		18.	C
9.	A		19.	B
10.	B		20.	B

EXAMINATION SECTION
TEST 1

DIRECTIONS: Each question or incomplete statement is followed by several suggested answers or completions. Select the one that BEST answers the question or completes the statement. *PRINT THE LETTER OF THE CORRECT ANSWER IN THE SPACE AT THE RIGHT.*

Questions 1-10.

DIRECTIONS: For each of the sentences given below, numbered 1 through 10, select from the following choices the MOST correct choice and print your choice in the space at the right. Select as your answer:
   A – if the statement contains an unnecessary word of expression
   B – if the statement contains a slang term or expression ordinarily not acceptable in government report writing
   C – if the statement contains an old-fashioned word or expression, where a concrete, plain term would be more useful
   D – if the statement contains no major faults

1. Every one of us should try harder.   1._____

2. Yours of the first instant has been received.   2._____

3. We will have to do a real snow job on him.   3._____

4. I shall contact him next Thursday.   4._____

5. None of us were invited to the meeting with the community.   5._____

6. We got this here job to do.   6._____

7. She could not help but see the mistake in the checkbook.   7._____

8. Don't bug the Director about the report.   8._____

9. I beg to inform you that your letter has been received.   9._____

10. This project is all screwed up.   10._____

Questions 11-15.

DIRECTIONS: Read the following Inter-office Memo. Then answer Questions 11 through 15 based ONLY on the memo.

INTER-OFFICE MEMORANDUM

To: Alma Robinson, Human Resources Aide
From: Frank Shields, Social Worker

I would like to have you help Mr. Edward Tunney who is trying to raise his two children by himself. He needs to learn to improve the physical care of his children and especially of his daughter Helen, age 9. She is avoided and ridiculed at school because her hair is uncombed, her teeth not properly cleaned, her clothing torn, wrinkled and dirty, as well as shabby and poorly fitted. The teachers and school officials have contacted the Department and the social worker for two years about Helen. She is not able to make friends because of these problems. I have talked to Mr. Tunney about improvements for the child's clothing, hair, and hygiene. He tends to deny these things are problems, but is cooperative, and a second person showing him the importance of better physical care for Helen would be helpful.

Perhaps you could teach Helen how to fix her own hair. She has all the materials. I would also like you to form your own opinion of the sanitary conditions in the home and how they could be improved.

Mr. Tunney is expecting your visit and is willing to talk with you about ways he can help with these problems.

11. In the above memorandum, the Human Resources Aide is being asked to help Mr. Tunney to   11._____

    A. improve the learning habits of his children
    B. enable his children to make friends at school
    C. take responsibility for the upbringing of his children
    D. give attention to the grooming and cleanliness of his children

12. This case was brought to the attention of the social worker by   12._____

    A. government officials
    B. teachers and school officials
    C. the Department
    D. Mr. Tunney

13. In general, Mr. Tunney's attitude with regard to his children could BEST be described as   13._____

    A. interested in correcting the obvious problems, but unable to do so alone
    B. unwilling to follow the advice of those who are trying to help
    C. concerned, but unaware of the seriousness of these problems
    D. interested in helping them, but afraid of taking the advice of the social worker

14. Which of the following actions has NOT been suggested as a possible step for the Human Resources Aide to take?   14._____

    A. Help Helen to learn to care for herself by teaching her grooming skills
    B. Determine ways of improvement through information gathered on a home visit
    C. Discuss her own views on Helen's problems with school officials
    D. Ask Mr. Tunney in what ways he believes the physical care may be improved

15. According to the memo, the Human Resources Aide is ESPECIALLY being asked to observe and form her own opinions about   15._____

    A.   the relationship between Mr. Tunney and the school officials
    B.   Helen's attitude toward her classmates and teacher
    C.   the sanitary conditions in the home
    D.   the reasons Mr. Tunney is not cooperative with the agency

16. In one day, an aide receives 18 inquiries by phone and 27 inquiries in person. What percentage of the inquiries received that day were by phone?   16._____

    A.   33%   B.   40%   C.   45%   D.   60%

17. If the weekly pay checks for 5 part-time employees are: $129.32, $162.74, $143.67, $135.75, and $156.56, then the combined weekly income for the 5 employees is   17._____

    A. $727.84   B. $728.04   C. $730.84   D. $737.04

18. Suppose that there are 17 aides working in an office where many community complaints are received by telephone. In one ten-day period, 4250 calls were received. If the same number of calls were received each day, and the aides divided the work load equally, about how many calls did each aide respond to daily?   18._____

    A.   25   B.   35   C.   75   D.   250

19. Suppose that an assignment was divided among 5 aides. If the first aide spent 67 hours on the assignment, the second aide spent 95 hours, the third aide spent 52 hours, the fourth aide spent 78 hours, and the fifth aide spent 103 hours, what was the AVERAGE amount of time spent by each aide on the assignment?   19._____
_____ hours.

    A.   71   B.   75   C.   79   D.   83

20. If there are 240 employees in a center and 1/3 are absent on the day of a bad snow-storm, how many employees were at work in the center on that day?   20._____

    A.   80   B.   120   C.   160   D.   200

KEY (CORRECT ANSWERS)

1.	D		11.	D
2.	C		12.	B
3.	B		13.	C
4.	D		14.	C
5.	D		15.	C
6.	B		16.	B
7.	D		17.	B
8.	B		18.	A
9.	C		19.	C
10.	B		20.	C

TEST 2

DIRECTIONS: Each question or incomplete statement is followed by several suggested answers or completions. Select the one that BEST answers the question or completes the statement. *PRINT THE LETTER OF THE CORRECT ANSWER IN THE SPACE AT THE RIGHT.*

1. Suppose that an aide takes 25 minutes to prepare a letter to a client.
   If the aide is assigned to prepare 9 letters on a certain day, how much time should she set aside for this task? _____ hours.

   A. 3 3/4   B. 4 1/4   C. 4 3/4   D. 5 1/4

   1.____

2. Suppose that a certain center uses both Form A and Form B in the course of its daily work, and that Form A is used 4 times as often as Form B.
   If the total number of both forms used in one week is 750, how many times was Form A used?

   A. 100   B. 200   C. 400   D. 600

   2.____

3. Suppose a center has a budget of $1092.70 from which 8 desks costing $78.05 apiece must be bought?
   How many ADDITIONAL desks can be ordered from this budget after the 8 desks have been purchased?

   A. 4   B. 6   C. 9   D. 14

   3.____

4. When researching a particular case, a team of 16 aides was asked to check through 234 folders to obtain the necessary information.
   If half the aides worked twice as fast as the other half, and the slow group checked through 12 folders each hour, about how long would it take to complete the assignment? _____ hours.

   A. $4\frac{1}{4}$ B. 5   C. 6   D. $6\frac{1}{2}$

   4.____

5. The difference in the cost of two printers is $28.32. If the less expensive printer costs $153.61, what is the cost of the other printer?

   A. $171.93   B. $172.03   C. $181.93   D. $182.03

   5.____

Questions 6-8.

DIRECTIONS: Questions 6 through 8 are to be answered on the basis of the following information contained on a sample page of a payroll book.

Emp. No.	Name of Employee	M	T	W	Th	F	Total Hours Worked	Pay PerHour	Total Wages
1	James Smith	8	8	8	8	8			$480.00
2	Gloria Jones	8	7 3/4	7	7 1/2			$16.00	$560.00
3	Robert Adams	6	6	71/2	71/2	8 3/4		$18.28	

122

6. The pay per hour of Employee No. 1 is   6.____

    A. $12.00   B. $13.72   C. $15.00   D. $19.20

7. The number of hours that Employee No. 2 worked on Friday is   7.____

    A. 4   B. 5 1/2   C. 4.63   D. 4 3/4

8. The total wages for Employee No. 3 is   8.____

    A. $636.92   B. $648.94   C. $661.04   D. $672.96

9. As a rule, the FIRST step in writing a check should be to   9.____

    A. number the check
    B. write in the payee's name
    C. tear out the check stub
    D. write the purpose of the check in the space provided at the bottom

10. If an error is made when writing a check, the MOST widely accepted procedure is to   10.____

    A. draw a line through the error and initial it
    B. destroy both the check and check stub by tearing into small pieces
    C. erase the error if it does not occur in the amount of the check
    D. write *Void* across both the check and check stub and save them

11. The check that is MOST easily cashed is one that is   11.____

    A. not signed   B. made payable to *Cash*
    C. post-dated   D. endorsed in part

12.   12.____

No. *103*	$ *142. 77*
May 14	
To *Alan Jacobs*	
For *Wages (5/6-5/10)*	
Bal. Bro't For'd	2340. 63
Amt. Deposited	205. 24
Total	
Amt. This Check	142. 77
Bal. Car'd For'd	

    The balance to be carried forward on the check stub above is
    A. $2,278.16   B. $1,992.62   C. $2,688.64   D. $2,403.10

13. The procedure for reconciling a bank statement consists of _____ the bank balance   13.____
    and _____ the checkbook balance.

    A. *adding* outstanding checks to; *subtracting* the service and check charges from
    B. *subtracting* the service charge from; *subtracting* outstanding checks from
    C. *subtracting* the service charge from; *adding* outstanding checks to
    D. *subtracting* outstanding checks from; *subtracting* the service and check charges
        from

14. An employee makes $15.70 an hour and receives time-and-a-half in overtime pay for every hour more than 40 in a given week. If the employee works 47 hours, the employee's total wages for that week would be

    A. $792.85   B. $837.90   C. $875.25   D. $1,106.85

14._____

15. A high-speed copier can make 25,000 copies before periodic service is required. Before this service is necessary, _____ copies of a 137-page document can be printed.

    A. 211   B. 204   C. 190   D. 178

15._____

16. An aide is typing a letter to the James Weldon Johnson Head Start Center. To be sure that a Mr. Joseph Maxwell reads it, an attention line is typed below the inside address. The salutation should, therefore, read:

    A. To Whom It May Concern: B. Dear Mr. Maxwell:
    C. Gentlemen: D. Dear Joseph:

16._____

17. When describing the advantages of the numeric filing system, it is NOT true that it

    A. is the most accurate of all methods
    B. allows for unlimited expansion according to the needs of the agency
    C. is a system useful for filing letters directly according to name or subject
    D. allows for cross-referencing

17._____

18. In writing a letter for your Center, the PURPOSE of the letter should usually be stated in

    A. the first paragraph. This assists the reader in making more sense of the letter.
    B. the second paragraph. The first paragraph should be used to confirm receipt of the letter being answered
    C. the last paragraph. The first paragraphs should be used to build up to the purpose of the letter.
    D. any paragraph. Each letter has a different purpose and the letter should conform to that purpose.

18._____

19. If you open a personal letter addressed to another aide by mistake, the one of the following actions which it would generally be BEST for you to take is to

    A. reseal the envelope or place the contents in another envelope and pass it on to the employee
    B. place the letter inside the envelope, indicate under your initials that it was opened in error and give it to the employee
    C. personally give the employee the letter without any explanation
    D. ignore your error, attach the envelope to the letter, and give it out in the usual manner

19._____

20. Of the following, the MAIN purpose of the head start program is to

    A. provide programs for pre-school development of children
    B. provide children between the ages of 6 and 12 with after-school activity
    C. establish a system for providing care for teenage youngsters with working parents
    D. supervise centers providing 24-hour child care

20._____

KEY (CORRECT ANSWERS)

1.	A	11.	B
2.	D	12.	D
3.	B	13.	D
4.	D	14.	A
5.	C	15.	D
6.	A	16.	C
7.	D	17.	C
8.	B	18.	A
9.	A	19.	B
10.	D	20.	A

———

EXAMINATION SECTION
TEST 1

DIRECTIONS: Each question or incomplete statement is followed by several suggested answers or completions. Select the one that *BEST* answers the question or completes the statement. *PRINT THE LETTER OF THE CORRECT ANSWER IN THE SPACE AT THE RIGHT.*

Questions 1-5.

DIRECTIONS: Each question from 1 to 5 consists of a sentence with an underlined word. For each question, select the choice that is *CLOSEST* in meaning to the underlined word.

EXAMPLE

This division reviews the <u>fiscal</u> reports of the agency.
In this sentence the word *fiscal* means most nearly
  A. financial   B. critical   C. basic   D. personnel
The correct answer is A. "financial" because "financial" is closest to *fiscal.* Therefore, the answer is A.

1. Every good office worker needs <u>basic</u> skills.
   The word *basic* in this sentence means

     A. fundamental   B. advanced   C. unusual   D. outstanding

1.____

2. He turned out to be a good <u>instructor</u>.
   The word *instructor* in this sentence means

     A. student   B. worker   C. typist   D. teacher

2.____

3. The <u>quantity</u> of work in the office was under study.
   In this sentence, the word *quantity* means

     A. amount   B. flow   C. supervision   D. type

3.____

4. The morning was spent <u>examining</u> the time records.
   In this sentence, the word *examining* means

     A. distributing   B. collecting   C. checking   D. filing

4.____

5. The candidate filled in the <u>proper</u> spaces on the form.
   In this sentence, the word *proper* means

     A. blank   B. appropriate   C. many   D. remaining

5.____

Questions 6-8.

DIRECTIONS: You are to answer Questions 6 through 8 *SOLELY* on the basis of the information contained in the following paragraph:

The increase in the number of public documents in the last two centuries closely matches the increase in population in the United States. The great number of public documents has become a serious threat to their usefulness. It is necessary to have programs which will reduce the number of public documents that are kept and which will, at the same time, assure keeping those that have value. Such programs need a great deal of thought to have any success.

6. According to the above paragraph, public documents may be less useful if 6.____

    A. the files are open to the public
    B. the record room is too small
    C. the copying machine is operated only during normal working hours
    D. too many records are being kept

7. According to the above paragraph, the growth of the population in the United States has matched the growth in the quantity of public documents for a period of, most nearly, 7.____

    A. 50 years   B. 100 years   C. 200 years   D. 300 years

8. According to the above paragraph, the increased number of public documents has made it necessary to 8.____

    A. find out which public documents are worth keeping
    B. reduce the great number of public documents by decreasing government services
    C. eliminate the copying of all original public documents
    D. avoid all new copying devices.

Questions 9-10.

DIRECTIONS: You are to answer Questions 9 and 10 *SOLELY* on the basis of the information contained in the following paragraph:

The work goals of an agency can best be reached if the employees understand and agree with these goals. One way to gain such understanding and agreement is for management to encourage and seriously consider suggestions from employees in the setting of agency goals.

9. On the basis of the paragraph above, the *BEST* way to achieve the work goals of an agency is to 9.____

    A. make certain that employees work as hard as possible
    B. study the organizational structure of the agency
    C. encourage employees to think seriously about the agency's problems
    D. stimulate employee understanding of the work goals

10. On the basis of the paragraph above, understanding and agreement with agency goals can be gained by 10.____

    A. allowing the employees to set agency goals
    B. reaching agency goals quickly
    C. legislative review of agency operations
    D. employee participation in setting agency goals

Questions 11-15.

DIRECTIONS: Each of Questions 11 through 15 consists of a group of four words. One word in each group is *INCORRECTLY* spelled. For each question, print the letter of the correct answer in the space at the right that is the same as the letter next to the word which is *INCORRECTLY* spelled.
EXAMPLE

    A. housing   B. certain   C. budgit   D. money

The word "budgit" is incorrectly spelled, because the correct spelling should be "budget." Therefore, the correct answer is C.

11.	A. sentince	B. bulletin	C. notice	D. definition	11._____
12.	A. appointment	B. exactly	C. typest	D. light	12._____
13.	A. penalty	B. suparvise	C. consider	D. division	13._____
14.	A. schedule	B. accurate	C. corect	D. simple	14._____
15.	A. suggestion	B. installed	C. proper	D. agincy	15._____

Questions 16-20.

DIRECTIONS: Each question from 16 through 20 consists of a sentence which may be
   A. incorrect because of bad word usage, or
   B. incorrect because of bad punctuation, or
   C. incorrect because of bad spelling, or
   D. correct
Read each sentence carefully. Then print in the proper space at the right A, B, C, or D, according to the answer you choose from the four choices listed above. There is only one type of error in each incorrect sentence. If there is no error, the sentence is correct.

EXAMPLE

George Washington was the father of his contry.
This sentence is incorrect because of bad spelling ("contry" instead of "country"). Therefore, the answer is C.

16. The assignment was completed in record time but the payroll for it has not yet been pre-parid.   16._____

17. The operator, on the other hand, is willing to learn me how to use the mimeograph.   17._____

18. She is the prettiest of the three sisters.   18._____

19. She doesn't know; if the mail has arrived.   19._____

20. The doorknob of the office door is broke.   20._____

21. A clerk can process a form in 15 minutes. How many forms can that clerk process in six hours?   21._____

   A. 10   B. 21   C. 24   D. 90

22. An office staff consists of 120 people. Sixty of them have been assigned to a special project. Of the remaining staff, 20 answer the mail, 10 handle phone calls, and the rest operate the office machines. The number of people operating the office machines is   22._____

   A. 20   B. 30   C. 40   D. 45

23. An office worker received 65 applications but on the first day had to return 26 of them for being incomplete and on the second day 25 had to be returned for being incomplete. How many applications did <u>not</u> have to be returned?   23._____

   A. 10   B. 12   C. 14   D. 16

24. An office worker answered 63 phone calls in one day and 91 phone calls the next day. For these 2 days, what was the average number of phone calls he answered per day?

    A. 77   B. 28   C. 82   D. 93

24.____

25. An office worker processed 12 vouchers of $8.75 each, 3 vouchers of $3.68 each, and 2 vouchers of $1.29 each. The total dollar amount of these vouchers is

    A. $116.04   B. $117.52   C. $118.62   D. $119.04

25.____

KEY (CORRECT ANSWERS)

1.	A		11.	A
2.	D		12.	C
3.	A		13.	B
4.	C		14.	C
5.	B		15.	D
6.	D		16.	C
7.	C		17.	A
8.	A		18.	D
9.	D		19.	B
10.	D		20.	A

21.	C
22.	B
23.	C
24.	A
25.	C

TEST 2

DIRECTIONS: Each question or incomplete statement is followed by several suggested answers or completions. Select the one that *BEST* answers the question or completes the statement. *PRINT THE LETTER OF THE CORRECT ANSWER IN THE SPACE AT THE RIGHT.*

Questions 1-5.

DIRECTIONS: Each question from 1 to 5 lists four names. The names may or may not be exactly the same. Compare the names in each question and mark your answer as follows:

Mark your answer A if all the names are different
Mark your answer B if only two names are exactly the same
Mark your answer C if only three names are exactly the same
Mark your answer D if all four names are exactly the same

EXAMPLE
Jensen, Alfred E.
Jensen, Alfred E.
Jensan, Alfred E.
Jensen, Fred E.

Since the name Jensen, Alfred E. appears twice and is exactly the same in both places, the correct answer is B.

1. Riviera, Pedro S.   1.____
   Rivers, Pedro S.
   Riviera, Pedro N.
   Riviera, Juan S.

2. Guider, Albert   2.____
   Guidar, Albert
   Giuder, Alfred
   Guider, Albert

3. Blum, Rona   3.____
   Blum, Rona
   Blum, Rona
   Blum, Rona

4. Raugh, John   4.____
   Raugh, James
   Raughe, John
   Raugh, John

5. Katz, Stanley   5.____
   Katz, Stanley
   Katze, Stanley
   Katz, Stanley

Questions 6-10.

DIRECTIONS: Each Question 6 through 10 consists of numbers or letters in Columns I and II.
For each question, compare each line of Column I with its corresponding line
in Column II and decide how many lines in Column I are EXACTLY the same
as their corresponding lines in Column II. In your answer space, mark your
answer as follows:

Mark your answer A if only ONE line in Column I is exactly the
same as its corresponding line in Column II
Mark your answer B if only TWO lines in Column I are exactly the
same as their corresponding lines in Column II
Mark your answer C if only THREE lines in Column I are exactly
the same as their corresponding lines in Column II
Mark your answer D if all FOUR lines in Column I are exactly the same as their corresponding lines in Column II

EXAMPLE

Column I	Column II
1776	1776
1865	1865
1945	1945
1976	1978

Only three lines in Column I are exactly the same as their corresponding lines in Column II.
Therefore, the correct answer is C.

	Column I	Column II	
6.	5653 8727 ZPSS 4952	5653 8728 ZPSS 9453	6._____
7.	PNJP NJPJ JNPN PNJP	PNPJ NJPJ JNPN PNPJ	7._____
8.	effe uWvw KpGj vmnv	eFfe uWvw KpGg vmnv	8._____
9.	5232 PfrC zssz rwwr	5232 PfrN zzss rwww	9._____
10.	czws cecc thrm lwtz	czws cece thrm lwtz	10._____

Questions 11-15.

DIRECTIONS: Questions 11 through 15 have lines of letters and numbers. Each letter should be matched with its number in accordance with the following table:

Letter	F	R	C	A	W	L	E	N	B	T
Matching Number	0	1	2	3	4	5	6	7	8	9

From the table you can determine that the letter F has the matching number 0 below it, the letter R has the matching number 1 below it, etc.

For each question, compare each line of letters and numbers carefully to see if each letter has its correct matching number. If all the letters and numbers are matched correctly in

none of the lines of the question, mark your answer A

only one of the lines of the question, mark your answer B

only two of the lines of the question, mark your answer C

all three lines of the question, mark your answer D

EXAMPLE
WBCR	4826
TLBF	9580
ATNE	3986

There is a mistake in the first line because the letter R should have its matching number 1 instead of the number 6.

The second line is correct because each letter shown has the correct matching number.

There is a mistake in the third line because the letter N should have the matching number 7 instead of the number 8,

Since all the letters and numbers are matched correctly in only one of the lines in the sample, the correct answer is B.

11.	EBCT	6829	11._____
	ATWR	3961	
	NLBW	7584	

12.	RNCT	1729	12._____
	LNCR	5728	
	WAEB	5368	

13.	NTWB	7948	13._____
	RABL	1385	
	TAEF	9360	

14.	LWRB	5417	14._____
	RLWN	1647	
	CBWA	2843	

15.	ABTC	3792	15._____
	WCER	5261	
	AWCN	3417	

16. Your job often brings you into contact with the public. Of the following, it would be *MOST*   16.____
desirable to explain the reasons for official actions to people coming into your office for
assistance because such explanations

    A. help build greater understanding between the public and your agency
    B. help build greater self-confidence in city employees
    C. convince the public that nothing they do can upset a city employee
    D. show the public that city employees are intelligent

17. Assume that you strongly dislike one of your co-workers.   17.____
You should *FIRST*

    A. discuss your feeling with the co-worker
    B. demand a transfer to another office
    C. suggest to your supervisor that the co-worker should be observed carefully
    D. try to figure out the reason for this dislike before you say or do anything

18. An office worker who has problems accepting authority is *MOST* likely to find it difficult to   18.____

    A. obey rules   B. understand people
    C. assist other employees   D. follow complex instructions

19. The employees in your office have taken a dislike to one person and frequently annoy   19.____
her. Your supervisor *should*

    A. transfer this person to another unit at the first opportunity
    B. try to find out the reason for the staff's attitude before doing anything about it
    C. threaten to transfer the first person observed bothering this person
    D. ignore the situation

20. Assume that your supervisor has asked a worker in your office to get a copy of a report   20.____
out of the files. You notice the worker has accidentally pulled out the wrong report.
Of the following, the *BEST* way for you to handle this situation is to tell

    A. the worker about all the difficulties that will result from this error
    B. the worker about her mistake in a nice way
    C. the worker to ignore this error
    D. your supervisor that this worker needs more training in how to use the files

21. Filing systems differ in their efficiency. Which of the following is the *BEST* way to evaluate   21.____
the efficiency of a filing system?
The

    A. number of times used per day
    B. amount of material that is received each day for filing
    C. amount of time it takes to locate material
    D. type of locking system used

22. In planning ahead so that a sufficient amount of general office supplies is always avail-   22.____
able, it would be *LEAST* important to find out the

    A. current office supply needs of the staff
    B. amount of office supplies used last year
    C. days and times that office supplies can be ordered
    D. agency goals and objectives

23. The *MAIN* reason for establishing routine office work procedures is that once a routine is established   23.____

    A. work need not be checked for accuracy
    B. all steps in the routine will take an equal amount of time to perform
    C. each time the job is repeated it will take less time to perform
    D. each step in the routine will not have to be planned all over again each time

24. When an office machine centrally located in an agency must be shut down for repairs, the bureaus and divisions using this machine should be informed of the   24.____

    A. expected length of time before the machine will be in operation again
    B. estimated cost of repairs
    C. efforts being made to avoid future repairs
    D. type of new equipment which the agency may buy in the future to replace the machine being repaired

25. If the day's work is properly scheduled, the *MOST* important result would be that the   25.____

    A. supervisor will not have to do much supervision
    B. employee will know what to do next
    C. employee will show greater initiative
    D. job will become routine

KEY (CORRECT ANSWERS)

1.	A	11.	C
2.	B	12.	B
3.	D	13.	D
4.	B	14.	B
5.	C	15.	A
6.	B	16.	A
7.	B	17.	D
8.	B	18.	A
9.	A	19.	B
10.	C	20.	B

21.	C
22.	D
23.	D
24.	A
25.	B

EXAMINATION SECTION
TEST 1

DIRECTIONS: Each question or incomplete statement is followed by several suggested answers or completions. Select the one that BEST answers the question or completes the statement. *PRINT THE LETTER OF THE CORRECT ANSWER IN THE SPACE AT THE RIGHT.*

1. Assume that a few co-workers meet near your desk and talk about personal matters during working hours. Lately, this practice has interfered with your work.
   In order to stop this practice, the BEST action for you to take FIRST is to

   A. ask your supervisor to put a stop to the co-workers' meeting near your desk
   B. discontinue any friendship with this group
   C. ask your co-workers not to meet near your desk
   D. request that your desk be moved to another location

   1.____

2. In order to maintain office coverage during working hours, your supervisor has scheduled your lunch hour from 1 P.M. to 2 P.M. and your co-worker's lunch hour from 12 P.M. to 1 P.M. Lately, your co-worker has been returning late from lunch each day. As a result, you don't get a full hour since you must return to the office by 2 P.M.
   Of the following, the BEST action for you to take FIRST is to

   A. explain to your co-worker in a courteous manner that his lateness is interfering with your right to a full hour for lunch
   B. tell your co-worker that his lateness must stop or you will report him to your supervisor
   C. report your co-worker's lateness to your supervisor
   D. leave at 1 P.M. for lunch, whether your co-worker has returned or not

   2.____

3. Assume that, as an office worker, one of your jobs is to open mail sent to your unit, read the mail for content, and send the mail to the appropriate person to handle. You accidentally open and begin to read a letter marked *personal* addressed to a co-worker.
   Of the following, the BEST action for you to take is to

   A. report to your supervisor that your co-worker is receiving personal mail at the office
   B. destroy the letter so that your co-worker does not know you saw it
   C. reseal the letter and place it on the co-worker's desk without saying anything
   D. bring the letter to your co-worker and explain that you opened it by accident

   3.____

4. Suppose that in evaluating your work, your supervisor gives you an overall good rating, but states that you sometimes turn in work with careless errors.
   The BEST action for you to take would be to

   A. ask a co-worker who is good at details to proofread your work
   B. take time to do a careful job, paying more attention to detail
   C. continue working as usual since occasional errors are to be expected
   D. ask your supervisor if she would mind correcting your errors

   4.____

5. Assume that you are taking a telephone message for a co-worker who is not in the office at the time.
   Of the following, the LEAST important item to write on the message is the

   A. length of the call   B. name of the caller
   C. time of the call   D. telephone number of the caller

   5.____

Questions 6-13.

DIRECTIONS: Questions 6 through 13 each consist of a sentence which may or may not be an example of good English. The underlined parts of each sentence may be correct or incorrect. Examine each sentence, considering grammar, punctuation, spelling, and capitalization. If the English usage in the underlined parts of the sentence given is better than any of the changes in the underlined words suggested in Options B, C, or D, choose Option A. If the changes in the underlined words suggested in Options B, C, or D would make the sentence correct, choose the correct option. Do not choose an option that will change the meaning of the sentence.

6. This Fall, the office will be closed on Columbus Day, October 9th.   6._____

   A. Correct as is
   B. fall...Columbus Day, October
   C. Fall...columbus day, October
   D. fall...Columbus Day, october

7. This manual discribes the duties performed by an Office Aide.   7._____

   A. Correct as is
   B. describe the duties performed
   C. discribe the duties performed
   D. describes the duties performed

8. There weren't no paper in the supply closet.   8._____

   A. Correct as is   B. weren't any
   C. wasn't any   D. wasn't no

9. The new employees left there office to attend a meeting.   9._____

   A. Correct as is   B. they're
   C. their   D. thier

10. The office worker started working at 8;30 a.m.   10._____

   A. Correct as is   B. 8:30 a.m.
   C. 8;30 a,m.   D. 8:30 am.

11. The alphabet, or A to Z sequence are the basis of most filing systems.   11._____

   A. Correct as is
   B. alphabet, or A to Z sequence, is
   C. alphabet, or A to Z sequence are
   D. alphabet, or A too Z sequence, is

12. Those file cabinets are five feet tall.   12._____

   A. Correct as is   B. Them...feet
   C. Those...foot   D. Them...foot

13. The Office Aide checked the <u>register and finding</u> the date of the meeting.   13.____

    A. Correct as is   B. regaster and finding
    C. register and found   D. regaster and found

Questions 14-21.

DIRECTIONS: Each of Questions 14 through 21 has two lists of numbers. Each list contains three sets of numbers. Check each of the three sets in the list on the right to see if they are the same as the corresponding set in the list on the left. Mark your answers:

    A. If none of the sets in the right list are the same as those in the left list
    B. if only one of the sets in the right list are the same as those in the left list
    C. if only two of the sets in the right list are the same as those in the left list
    D. if all three sets in the right list are the same as those in the left list

14. 7354183476   7354983476   14.____
    4474747744   4474747774
    57914302311   57914302311

15. 7143592185   7143892185   15.____
    8344517699   8344518699
    9178531263   9178531263

16. 2572114731   257214731   16.____
    8806835476   8806835476
    8255831246   8255831246

17. 331476853821   331476858621   17.____
    6976658532996   6976655832996
    3766042113715   3766042113745

18. 8806663315   8806663315   18.____
    74477138449   74477138449
    211756663666   211756663666

19. 990006966996   99000696996   19.____
    53022219743   53022219843
    4171171117717   4171171177717

20. 24400222433004   24400222433004   20.____
    5300030055000355   5300030055500355
    20000075532002022   20000075532002022

21. 611166640660001116   61116664066001116   21.____
    7111300117001100733   7111300117001100733
    26666446664476518   26666446664476518

Questions 22-25.

DIRECTIONS: Each of Questions 22 through 25 has two lists of names and addresses. Each
list contains three sets of names and addresses. Check each of the three sets
in the list on the right to see if they are the same as the corresponding set in
the list on the left. Mark your answers:
A.   if none of the sets in the right list are the same as those in the left
list
B.   if only one of the sets in the right list is the same as those in the left
list
C.   if only two of the sets in the right list are the same as those in the
left list
D.   if all three sets in the right list are the same as those in the left list

22.   Mary T. Berlinger
2351 Hampton St.
Monsey, N.Y. 20117

Eduardo Benes
473 Kingston Avenue
Central Islip, N.Y. 11734

Alan Carrington Fuchs
17 Gnarled Hollow Road
Los Angeles, CA 91635

Mary T. Berlinger
2351 Hampton St.
Monsey, N.Y. 20117

Eduardo Benes
473 Kingston Avenue
Central Islip, N.Y. 11734

Alan Carrington Fuchs
17 Gnarled Hollow Road
Los Angeles, CA 91685

22._____

23.   David John Jacobson
178 35 St. Apt. 4C
New York, N.Y. 00927

Ann-Marie Calonella
7243 South Ridge Blvd.
Bakersfield, CA 96714

Pauline M. Thompson
872 Linden Ave.
Houston, Texas 70321

David John Jacobson
178 53 St. Apt. 4C
New York, N.Y. 00927

Ann-Marie Calonella
7243 South Ridge Blvd.
Bakersfield, CA 96714

Pauline M. Thomson
872 Linden Ave.
Houston, Texas 70321

23._____

24.   Chester LeRoy Masterton
152 Lacy Rd.
Kankakee, Ill. 54532

William Maloney
S. LaCrosse Pla.
Wausau, Wisconsin 52146

Cynthia V. Barnes
16 Pines Rd.
Greenpoint, Miss. 20376

Chester LeRoy Masterson
152 Lacy Rd.
Kankakee, Ill. 54532

William Maloney
S. LaCross Pla.
Wausau, Wisconsin 52146

Cynthia V. Barnes
16 Pines Rd.
Greenpoint, Miss. 20376

24._____

25. Marcel Jean Frontenac
6 Burton On The Water
Calender, Me. 01471

J. Scott Marsden
174 S. Tipton St.
Cleveland, Ohio

Lawrence T. Haney
171 McDonough St.
Decatur, Ga. 31304

Marcel Jean Frontenac
6 Burton On The Water
Calender, Me. 01471

J. Scott Marsden
174 Tipton St.
Cleveland, Ohio

Lawrence T. Haney
171 McDonough St.
Decatur, Ga. 31304

25._____

———

KEY (CORRECT ANSWERS)

1.	C		11.	B
2.	A		12.	A
3.	D		13.	C
4.	B		14.	B
5.	A		15.	B
6.	A		16.	C
7.	D		17.	A
8.	C		18.	D
9.	C		19.	A
10.	B		20.	C

21.	C
22.	C
23.	B
24.	B
25.	C

———

TEST 2

Questions 1-6.

DIRECTIONS: Questions 1 through 6 are to be answered SOLELY on the basis of the information contained in the following passage.

Duplicating is the process of making a number of identical copies of letters, documents, etc. from an original. Some duplicating processes make copies directly from the original document. Other duplicating processes require the preparation of a special master, and copies are then made from the master. Four of the most common duplicating processes are stencil, fluid, offset, and xerox.

In the stencil process, the typewriter is used to cut the words into a master called a stencil. Drawings, charts, or graphs can be cut into the stencil using a stylus. As many as 3,500 good-quality copies can be reproduced from one stencil. Various grades of finished paper from inexpensive mimeograph to expensive bond can be used.

The fluid process is a good method of copying from 50 to 125 good-quality copies from a master, which is prepared with a special dye. The master is placed on the duplicator, and special paper with a hard finish is moistened and then passed through the duplicator. Some of the dye on the master is dissolved, creating an impression on the paper. The impression becomes lighter as more copies are made; and once the dye on the master is used up, a new master must be made.

The offset process is the most adaptable office duplicating process because this process can be used for making a few copies or many copies. Masters can be made on paper or plastic for a few hundred copies, or on metal plates for as many as 75,000 copies. By using a special technique called photo-offset, charts, photographs, illustrations, or graphs can be reproduced on the master plate. The offset process is capable of producing large quantities of fine, top-quality copies on all types of finished paper.

The xerox process reproduces an exact duplicate from an original. It is the fastest duplicating method because the original material is placed directly on the duplicator, eliminating the need to make a special master. Any kind of paper can be used. The xerox process is the most expensive duplicating process; however, it is the best method of reproducing small quantities of good-quality copies of reports, letters, official documents, memos, or contracts.

1. Of the following, the MOST efficient method of reproducing 5,000 copies of a graph is   1.____

   A. stencil   B. fluid   C. offset   D. xerox

2. The offset process is the MOST adaptable office duplicating process because   2.____

   A. it is the quickest duplicating method
   B. it is the least expensive duplicating method
   C. it can produce a small number or large number of copies
   D. a softer master can be used over and over again

3. Which one of the following duplicating processes uses moistened paper? 3.____

   A. Stencil   B. Fluid   C. Offset   D. Xerox

4. The fluid process would be the BEST process to use for reproducing 4.____

   A. five copies of a school transcript
   B. fifty copies of a memo
   C. five hundred copies of a form letter
   D. five thousand copies of a chart

5. Which one of the following duplicating processes does NOT require a special master? 5.____

   A. Fluid   B. Xerox   C. Offset   D. Stencil

6. Xerox is NOT used for all duplicating jobs because 6.____

   A. it produces poor-quality copies
   B. the process is too expensive
   C. preparing the master is too time-consuming
   D. it cannot produce written reports

7. Assume a city agency has 775 office workers.
   If 2 out of 25 office workers were absent on a particular day, how many office workers reported to work on that day? 7.____

   A. 713   B. 744   C. 750   D. 773

Questions 8-11.

DIRECTIONS: In Questions 8 through 11, select the choice that is CLOSEST in meaning to the underlined word.

SAMPLE: This division reviews the fiscal reports of the agency.
In this sentence, the word fiscal means MOST NEARLY
    A. financial   B. critical   C. basic   D. personnel

    The correct answer is A, financial, because financial is closest to fiscal.

8. A central file eliminates the need to retain duplicate material.
   The word retain means MOST NEARLY 8.____

   A. keep   B. change   C. locate   D. process

9. Filing is a routine office task.
   Routine means MOST NEARLY 9.____

   A. proper   B. regular   C. simple   D. difficult

10. Sometimes a word, phrase, or sentence must be deleted to correct an error. 10.____
    Deleted means MOST NEARLY

    A. removed   B. added   C. expanded   D. improved

11. Your supervisor will <u>evaluate</u> your work.
    <u>Evaluate</u> means MOST NEARLY

    A. judge   B. list   C. assign   D. explain

Questions 12-19.

DIRECTIONS: The code table below shows 10 letters with matching numbers. For each Question 12 through 19, there are three sets of letters. Each set of letters is followed by a set of numbers which may or may not match their correct letter according to the code table. For each question, check all three sets of letters and numbers and mark your answer:

    A.   if no pairs are correctly matched
    B.   if only one pair is correctly matched
    C.   if only two pairs are correctly matched
    D.   if all three pairs are correctly matched

<u>CODE TABLE</u>

T	M	V	D	S	P	R	G	B	H
1	2	3	4	5	6	7	8	9	0

<u>Sample Question:</u>   TMVDSP - 123456
                        RGBHTM - 789011
                        DSPRGB - 256789

In the sample question above, the first set of numbers correctly matches its set of letters. But the second and third pairs contain mistakes. In the second pair, M is incorrectly matched with number 1. According to the code table, letter M should be correctly matched with number 2. In the third pair, the letter D is incorrectly matched with number 2. According to the code table, letter D should be correctly matched with number 4. Since only one of the pairs is correctly matched, the answer to this sample question is B.

12. RSBMRM - 759262
      GDSRVH - 845730
      VDBRTM - 349713

13. TGVSDR - 183247
      SMHRDP - 520647
      TRMHSR - 172057

14. DSPRGM - 456782
      MVDBHT - 234902
      HPMDBT - 062491

15. BVPTRD - 936184
      GDPHMB - 807029
      GMRHMV - 827032

16. MGVRSH - 283750
      TRDMBS - 174295
      SPRMGV - 567283

17. SGBSDM - 489542
    MGHPTM - 290612
    MPBMHT - 269301

   17._____

18. TDPBHM - 146902
    VPBMRS - 369275
    GDMBHM - 842902

   18._____

19. MVPTBV - 236194
    PDRTMB - 647128
    BGTMSM - 981232

   19._____

Questions 20-25.

DIRECTIONS: In each of Questions 20 through 25, the names of four people are given. For each question, choose as your answer the one of the four names given which should be filed FIRST according to the usual system of alphabetical filing of names, as described in the following paragraph.

In filing names, you must start with the last name. Names are filed in order of the first letter of the last name, then the second letter, etc. Therefore, BAILY would be filed before BROWN, which would be filed before COLT. A name with fewer letters of the same type comes first; i.e., Smith before Smithe. If the last names are the same, the names are filed alphabetically by the first name. If the first name is an initial, a name with an initial would come before a first name that starts with the same letter as the initial. Therefore, I. BROWN would come before IRA BROWN. Finally, if both last name and first name are the same, the name would be filed alphabetically by the middle name, one again an initial coming before a middle name which starts with the same letter as the initial. If there is no middle name at all, the name would come before those with middle initials or names.

Sample Question: A. Lester Daniels
                  B. William Dancer
                  C. Nathan Danzig
                  D. Dan Lester

The last names beginning with D are filed before the last name beginning with L. Since DANIELS, DANCER, and DANZIG all begin with the same three letters, you must look at the fourth letter of the last name to determine which name should be filed first. C comes before I or Z in the alphabet, so DANCER is filed before DANIELS or DANZIG. Therefore, the answer to the above sample question is B.

20.   A. Scott Biala   B. Mary Byala   20._____
     C. Martin Baylor   D. Francis Bauer

21.   A. Howard J. Black   B. Howard Black   21._____
     C. J. Howard Black   D. John H. Black

22.   A. Theodora Garth Kingston   B. Theadore Barth Kingston   22._____
     C. Thomas Kingston   D. Thomas T. Kingston

23.   A. Paulette Mary Huerta   B. Paul M. Huerta   23._____
     C. Paulette L. Huerta   D. Peter A. Huerta

24.   A. Martha Hunt Morgan   B. Martin Hunt Morgan   24.____
        C. Mary H. Morgan   D. Martine H. Morgan

25.   A. James T. Meerschaum   B. James M. Mershum   25.____
        C. James F. Mearshaum   D. James N. Meshum

KEY (CORRECT ANSWERS)

1.	C	11.	A
2.	C	12.	B
3.	B	13.	B
4.	B	14.	C
5.	B	15.	A
6.	B	16.	D
7.	A	17.	A
8.	A	18.	D
9.	B	19.	A
10.	A	20.	D

21.	B
22.	B
23.	B
24.	A
25.	C

TEST 3

DIRECTIONS: Each question or incomplete statement is followed by several suggested answers or completions. Select the one that BEST answers the question or completes the statement. *PRINT THE LETTER OF THE CORRECT ANSWER IN THE SPACE AT THE RIGHT.*

1. Which one of the following statements about proper telephone usage is NOT always correct?
   When answering the telephone, you should

   A. know whom you are speaking to
   B. give the caller your undivided attention
   C. identify yourself to the caller
   D. obtain the information the caller wishes before you do your other work

   1.____

2. Assume that, as a member of a worker's safety committee in your agency, you are responsible for encouraging other employees to follow correct safety practices. While you are working on your regular assignment, you observe an employee violating a safety rule.
   Of the following, the BEST action for you to take FIRST is to

   A. speak to the employee about safety practices and order him to stop violating the safety rule
   B. speak to the employee about safety practices and point out the safety rule he is violating
   C. bring the matter up in the next committee meeting
   D. report this violation of the safety rule to the employee's supervisor

   2.____

3. Assume that you have been temporarily assigned by your supervisor to do a job which you do not want to do. The BEST action for you to take is to

   A. discuss the job with your supervisor, explaining why you do not want to do it
   B. discuss the job with your supervisor and tell her that you will not do it
   C. ask a co-worker to take your place on this job
   D. do some other job that you like; your supervisor may give the job you do not like to someone else

   3.____

4. Assume that you keep the confidential personnel files of employees in your unit. A friend asks you to obtain some information from the file of one of your co-workers.
   The BEST action to take is to _____ to your friend.

   A. ask the co-worker if you can give the information
   B. ask your supervisor if you can give the information
   C. give the information
   D. refuse to give the information

   4.____

Questions 5-8.

DIRECTIONS: Questions 5 through 8 are to be answered SOLELY on the basis of the information contained in the following passage.

City government is committed to providing a safe and healthy work environment for all city employees. An effective agency safety program reduces accidents by educating employees about the types of careless acts which can cause accidents. Even in an office, accidents can happen. If each employee is aware of possible safety hazards, the number of accidents on the job can be reduced.

Careless use of office equipment can cause accidents and injuries. For example, file cabinet drawers which are filled with papers can be so heavy that the entire cabinet could tip over from the weight of one open drawer.

The bottom drawers of desks and file cabinets should never be left open since employees could easily trip over open drawers and injure themselves.

When reaching for objects on a high shelf, an employee should use a strong, sturdy object such as a step stool to stand on. Makeshift platforms made out of books, papers, or boxes can easily collapse. Even chairs can slide out from under foot, causing serious injury.

Even at an employee's desk, safety hazards can occur. Frayed or cut wires should be repaired or replaced immediately. Computers which are not firmly anchored to the desk or table could fall, causing injury.

Smoking is one of the major causes of fires in the office. A lighted match or improperly extinguished cigarette thrown into a wastebasket filled with paper could cause a major fire with possible loss of life. Where smoking is permitted, ashtrays should be used. Smoking is particularly dangerous in offices where flammable chemicals are used.

5. The goal of an effective safety program is to   5._____

    A.   reduce office accidents
    B.   stop employees from smoking on the job
    C.   encourage employees to continue their education
    D.   eliminate high shelves in offices

6. Desks and file cabinets can become safety hazards when   6._____

    A.   their drawers are left open
    B.   they are used as wastebaskets
    C.   they are makeshift
    D.   they are not anchored securely to the floor

7. Smoking is especially hazardous when it occurs   7._____

    A.   near exposed wires
    B.   in a crowded office
    C.   in an area where flammable chemicals are used
    D.   where books and papers are stored

8. Accidents are likely to occur when   8._____

    A.   employees' desks are cluttered with books and papers
    B.   employees are not aware of safety hazards
    C.   employees close desk drawers
    D.   step stools are used to reach high objects

9. Assume that part of your job as a worker in the accounting division of a city agency is to answer the telephone. When you first answer the telephone, it is LEAST important to tell the caller

    A. your title
    B. your name
    C. the name of your unit
    D. the name of your agency

9._____

10. Assume that you are assigned to work as a receptionist, and your duties are to answer phones, greet visitors, and do other general office work. You are busy with a routine job when several visitors approach your desk.
The BEST action to take is to

    A. ask the visitors to have a seat and assist them after your work is completed
    B. tell the visitors that you are busy and they should return at a more convenient time
    C. stop working long enough to assist the visitors
    D. continue working and wait for the visitors to ask you for assistance

10._____

11. Assume that your supervisor has chosen you to take a special course during working hours to learn a new payroll procedure. Although you know that you were chosen because of your good work record, a co-worker, who feels that he should have been chosen, has been telling everyone in your unit that the choice was unfair.
Of the following, the BEST way to handle this situation FIRST is to

    A. suggest to the co-worker that everything in life is unfair
    B. contact your union representative in case your co-worker presents a formal grievance
    C. tell your supervisor about your co-worker's complaints and let her handle the situation
    D. tell the co-worker that you were chosen because of your superior work record

11._____

12. Assume that while you are working on an assignment which must be completed quickly, a supervisor from another unit asks you to obtain information for her.
Of the following, the BEST way to respond to her request is to

    A. tell her to return in an hour since you are busy
    B. give her the names of some people in her own unit who could help her
    C. tell her you are busy and refer her to a co-worker
    D. tell her that you are busy and ask her if she could wait until you finish your assignment

12._____

13. A co-worker in your unit is often off from work because of illness. Your supervisor assigns the co-worker's work to you when she is not there. Lately, doing her work has interfered with your own job.
The BEST action for you to take FIRST is to

    A. discuss the problem with your supervisor
    B. complete your own work before starting your co-worker's work
    C. ask other workers in your unit to assist you
    D. work late in order to get the jobs done

13._____

14. During the month of June, 40,587 people attended a city-owned swimming pool. In July, 13,014 more people attended the swimming pool than the number that had attended in June. In August, 39,655 people attended the swimming pool.
The TOTAL number of people who attended the swimming pool during the months of June, July, and August was

14._____

    A. 80,242   B. 93,256   C. 133,843   D. 210,382

Questions 15-22.

DIRECTIONS: Questions 15 through 22 test how well you understand what you read. It will be necessary for you to read carefully because your answers to these questions must be based ONLY on the information in the following paragraphs.

The telephone directory is made up of two books. The first book consists of the introductory section and the alphabetical listing of names section. The second book is the classified directory (also known as the yellow pages). Many people who are familiar with one book do not realize how useful the other can be. The efficient office worker should become familiar with both books in order to make the best use of this important source of information.

The introductory section gives general instructions for finding numbers in the alphabetical listing and classified directory. This section also explains how to use the telephone company's many services, including the operator and information services, gives examples of charges for local and long-distance calls, and lists area codes for the entire country. In addition, this section provides a useful postal zip code map.

The alphabetical listing of names section lists the names, addresses, and telephone numbers of subscribers in an area. Guide names, or *telltales,* are on the top corner of each page. These guide names indicate the first and last name to be found on that page. *Telltales* help locate any particular name quickly. A cross-reference spelling is also given to help locate names which are spelled several different ways. City, state, and federal government agencies are listed under the major government heading. For example, an agency of the federal government would be listed under *United States Government.*

The classified directory, or yellow pages, is a separate book. In this section are advertising services, public transportation line maps, shopping guides, and listings of businesses arranged by the type of product or services they offer. This book is most useful when looking for the name or phone number of a business when all that is known is the type of product offered and the address, or when trying to locate a particular type of business in an area. Businesses listed in the classified directory can usually be found in the alphabetical listing of names section. When the name of the business is known, you will find the address or phone number more quickly in the alphabetical listing of names section.

15. The introductory section provides

15._____

    A. shopping guides   B. government listings
    C. business listings   D. information services

16. Advertising services would be found in the

16._____

    A. introductory section   B. alphabetical listing of names section
    C. classified directory   D. information services

17. According to the information in the above passage for locating government agencies, the Information Office of the Department of Consumer Affairs of New York City government would be alphabetically listed FIRST under

    A. *I* for Information Offices
    B. *D* for Department of Consumer Affairs
    C. *N* for New York City
    D. *G* for government

17.____

18. When the name of a business is known, the QUICKEST way to find the phone number is to look in the

    A. classified directory
    B. introductory section
    C. alphabetical listing of names section
    D. advertising service section

18.____

19. The QUICKEST way to find the phone number of a business when the type of service a business offers and its address is known is to look in the

    A. classified directory
    B. alphabetical listing of names section
    C. introductory section
    D. information service

19.____

20. What is a *telltale*?

    A. An alphabetical listing
    B. A guide name
    C. A map
    D. A cross-reference listing

20.____

21. The BEST way to find a postal zip code is to look in the

    A. classified directory
    B. introductory section
    C. alphabetical listing of names section
    D. government heading

21.____

22. To help find names which have several different spellings, the telephone directory provides

    A. cross-reference spelling
    B. *telltales*
    C. spelling guides
    D. advertising services

22.____

23. Assume that your agency has been given $2025 to purchase file cabinets. If each file cabinet costs $135, how many file cabinets can your agency purchase?

    A. 8   B. 10   C. 15   D. 16

23.____

24. Assume that your unit ordered 14 staplers at a total cost of $30.20, and each stapler cost the same.
The cost of one stapler was MOST NEARLY

    A. $1.02   B. $1.61   C. $2.16   D. $2.26

24.____

25. Assume that you are responsible for counting and recording licensing fees collected by your department. On a particular day, your department collected in fees 40 checks in the amount of $6 each, 80 checks in the amount of $4 each, 45 twenty dollar bills, 30 ten dollar bills, 42 five dollar bills, and 186 one dollar bills.
The TOTAL amount in fees collected on that day was

    A. $1,406   B. $1,706   C. $2,156   D. $2,356

25.____

26. Assume that you are responsible for your agency's petty cash fund. During the month of February, you pay out 7 $2.00 subway fares and one taxi fare for $10.85. You pay out nothing else from the fund. At the end of February, you count the money left in the fund and find 3 one dollar bills, 4 quarters, 5 dimes, and 4 nickels. The amount of money you had available in the petty cash fund at the BEGINNING of February was

    A. $4.70   B. $16.35   C. $24.85   D. $29.55

26.____

27. You overhear your supervisor criticize a co-worker for handling equipment in an unsafe way. You feel that the criticism may be unfair.
Of the following, it would be BEST for you to

    A. take your co-worker aside and tell her how you feel about your supervisor's comments
    B. interrupt the discussion and defend your co-worker to your supervisor
    C. continue working as if you had not overheard the discussion
    D. make a list of other workers who have violated safety rules and give it to your supervisor

27.____

28. Assume that you have been assigned to work on a long-term project with an employee who is known for being uncooperative.
In beginning to work with this employee, it would be LEAST desirable for you to

    A. understand why the person is uncooperative
    B. act in a calm manner rather than an emotional manner
    C. be appreciative of the co-worker's work
    D. report the co-worker's lack of cooperation to your supervisor

28.____

29. Assume that you are assigned to sell tickets at a city-owned ice skating rink. An adult ticket costs $4.50, and a children's ticket costs $2.25. At the end of a day, you find that you have sold 36 adult tickets and 80 children's tickets.
The TOTAL amount of money you collected for that day was

    A. $244.80   B. $318.00   C. $342.00   D. $348.00

29.____

30. If each office worker files 487 index cards in one hour, how many cards can 26 office workers file in one hour?

    A. 10,662   B. 12,175   C. 12,662   D. 14,266

30.____

KEY (CORRECT ANSWERS)

1.	D	16.	C
2.	B	17.	C
3.	A	18.	C
4.	D	19.	A
5.	A	20.	B
6.	A	21.	B
7.	C	22.	A
8.	B	23.	C
9.	A	24.	C
10.	C	25.	C
11.	C	26.	D
12.	D	27.	C
13.	A	28.	D
14.	C	29.	C
15.	D	30.	C

PREPARING WRITTEN MATERIAL

PARAGRAPH REARRANGEMENT
COMMENTARY

The sentences which follow are in scrambled order. You are to rearrange them in proper order and indicate the letter choice containing the correct answer at the space at the right.

Each group of sentences in this section is actually a paragraph presented in scrambled order. Each sentence in the group has a place in that paragraph; no sentence is to be left out. You are to read each group of sentences and decide upon the best order in which to put the sentences so as to form as well-organized paragraph.

The questions in this section measure the ability to solve a problem when all the facts relevant to its solution are not given.

More specifically, certain positions of responsibility and authority require the employee to discover connections between events sometimes, apparently, unrelated. In order to do this, the employee will find it necessary to correctly infer that unspecified events have probably occurred or are likely to occur. This ability becomes especially important when action must be taken on incomplete information.

Accordingly, these questions require competitors to choose among several suggested alternatives, each of which presents a different sequential arrangement of the events. Competitors must choose the MOST logical of the suggested sequences.

In order to do so, they may be required to draw on general knowledge to infer missing concepts or events that are essential to sequencing the given events. Competitors should be careful to infer only what is essential to the sequence. The plausibility of the wrong alternatives will always require the inclusion of unlikely events or of additional chains of events which are NOT essential to sequencing the given events.

It's very important to remember that you are looking for the best of the four possible choices, and that the best choice of all may not even be one of the answers you're given to choose from.

There is no one right way to solve these problems. Many people have found it helpful to first write out the order of the sentences, as they would have arranged them, on their scrap paper before looking at the possible answers. If their optimum answer is there, this can save them some time. If it isn't, this method can still give insight into solving the problem. Others find it most helpful to just go through each of the possible choices, contrasting each as they go along. You should use whatever method feels comfortable, and works, for you.

While most of these types of questions are not that difficult, we've added a higher percentage of the difficult type, just to give you more practice. Usually there are only one or two questions on this section that contain such subtle distinctions that you're unable to answer confidently, and you then may find yourself stuck deciding between two possible choices, neither of which you're sure about.

EXAMINATION SECTION
TEST 1

DIRECTIONS: The sentences that follow are in scrambled order. You are to rearrange them in proper order and indicate the letter choice containing the correct answer. *PRINT THE LETTER OF THE CORRECT ANSWER IN THE SPACE AT THE RIGHT.*

1. Below are four statements labeled W., X., Y., and Z.   1.____

    W.   He was a strict and fanatic drillmaster.

    X.   The word is always used in a derogatory sense and generally shows resentment and anger on the part of the user.

    Y.   It is from the name of this Frenchman that we derive our English word, martinet.

    Z.   Jean Martinet was the Inspector-General of Infantry during the reign of King Louis XIV.

The *PROPER* order in which these sentences should be placed in a paragraph is:

  A. X, Z, W, Y   B. X, Z, Y, W   C. Z, W, Y, X   D. Z, Y, W, X

2. In the following paragraph, the sentences which are numbered, have been jumbled.   2.____

    1.   Since then it has undergone changes.

    2.   It was incorporated in 1955 under the laws of the State of New York.

    3.   Its primary purpose, a cleaner city, has, however, remained the same.

    4.   The Citizens Committee works in cooperation with the Mayor's Inter-departmental Committee for a Clean City.

The order in which these sentences should be arranged to form a well-organized paragraph is:

  A. 2, 4, 1, 3   B. 3, 4, 1, 2   C. 4, 2, 1, 3   D. 4, 3, 2, 1

Questions 3-5.

DIRECTIONS: The sentences listed below are part of a meaningful paragraph but they are not given in their proper order. You are to decide what would be the *best order* in which to put the sentences so as to form a well-organized paragraph. Each sentence has a place in the paragraph; there are no extra sentences. You are then to answer questions 3 to 5 inclusive on the basis of your rearrangements of these scrambled sentences into a properly organized paragraph.

In 1887 some insurance companies organized an Inspection Department to advise their clients on all phases of fire prevention and protection. Probably this has been due to the smaller annual fire losses in Great Britain than in the United States. It tests various fire prevention devices and appliances and determines manufacturing hazards and their safeguards. Fire research began earlier in the United States and is more advanced than in Great Britain. Later they established a laboratory specializing in electrical, mechanical, hydraulic, and chemical fields.

3. When the five sentences are arranged in proper order, the paragraph starts with the sentence which begins

    A. "In 1887 ..."   B. "Probably this ..."   C. "It tests ..."
    D. "Fire research ..."   E. "Later they ..."

3.____

4. In the last sentence listed above, "they" refers to

    A. insurance companies
    B. the United States and Great Britain
    C. the Inspection Department
    D. clients
    E. technicians

4.____

5. When the above paragraph is properly arranged, it ends with the words

    A. "... and protection."   B. "... the United States."
    C. "... their safeguards."   D. "... in Great Britain."
    E. "... chemical fields."

5.____

KEY (CORRECT ANSWERS)

1. C
2. C
3. D
4. A
5. C

TEST 2

DIRECTIONS: In each of the questions numbered 1 through 5, several sentences are given. For each question, choose as your answer the group of numbers that represents the *most logical* order of these sentences if they were arranged in paragraph form. *PRINT THE LETTER OF THE CORRECT ANSWER IN THE SPACE AT THE RIGHT.*

1.
1. It is established when one shows that the landlord has prevented the tenant's enjoyment of his interest in the property leased.
2. Constructive eviction is the result of a breach of the covenant of quiet enjoyment implied in all leases.
3. In some parts of the United States, it is not complete until the tenant vacates within a reasonable time.
4. Generally, the acts must be of such serious and permanent character as to deny the tenant the enjoyment of his possessing rights.
5. In this event, upon abandonment of the premises, the tenant's liability for that ceases.

The CORRECT answer is:

A. 2, 1, 4, 3, 5   B. 5, 2, 3, 1, 4   C. 4, 3, 1, 2, 5
D. 1, 3, 5, 4, 2

1._____

2.
1. The powerlessness before private and public authorities that is the typical experience of the slum tenant is reminiscent of the situation of blue-collar workers all through the nineteenth century.
2. Similarly, in recent years, this chapter of history has been reopened by anti-poverty groups which have attempted to organize slum tenants to enable them to bargain collectively with their landlords about the conditions of their tenancies.
3. It is familiar history that many of the workers remedied their condition by joining together and presenting their demands collectively.
4. Like the workers, tenants are forced by the conditions of modern life into substantial dependence on these who possess great political arid economic power.
5. What's more, the very fact of dependence coupled with an absence of education and self-confidence makes them hesitant and unable to stand up for what they need from those in power.

The CORRECT answer is:

A. 5, 4, 1, 2, 3   B. 2, 3, 1, 5, 4   C. 3, 1, 5, 4, 2
D. 1, 4, 5, 3, 2

2._____

3.
1. A railroad, for example, when not acting as a common carrier may contract away responsibility for its own negligence.
2. As to a landlord, however, no decision has been found relating to the legal effect of a clause shifting the statutory duty of repair to the tenant.
3. The courts have not passed on the validity of clauses relieving the landlord of this duty and liability.
4. They have, however, upheld the validity of exculpatory clauses in other types of contracts.
5. Housing regulations impose a duty upon the landlord to maintain leased premises in safe condition.

3._____

6. As another example, a bailee may limit his liability except for gross negligence, willful acts, or fraud.

The CORRECT answer is:

A. 2, 1, 6, 4, 3, 5　　　B. 1, 3, 4, 5, 6, 2　　　C. 3, 5, 1, 4, 2, 6
D. 5, 3, 4, 1, 6, 2

4. 1. Since there are only samples in the building, retail or consumer sales are generally eschewed by mart occupants, and in some instances, rigid controls are maintained to limit entrance to the mart only to those persons engaged in retailing.
　2. Since World War I, in many larger cities, there has developed a new type of property, called the mart building.
　3. It can, therefore, be used by wholesalers and jobbers for the display of sample merchandise.
　4. This type of building is most frequently a multi-storied, finished interior property which is a cross between a retail arcade and a loft building.
　5. This limitation enables the mart occupants to ship the orders from another location after the retailer or dealer makes his selection from the samples.

The CORRECT answer is:

4.____

A. 2, 4, 3, 1, 5　　　B. 4, 3, 5, 1, 2　　　C. 1, 3, 2, 4, 5
D. 1, 4, 2, 3, 5

5. 1. In general, staff-line friction reduces the distinctive contribution of staff personnel.
　2. The conflicts, however, introduce an uncontrolled element into the managerial system.
　3. On the other hand, the natural resistance of the line to staff innovations probably usefully restrains over-eager efforts to apply untested procedures on a large scale.
　4. Under such conditions, it is difficult to know when valuable ideas are being sacrificed.
　5. The relatively weak position of staff, requiring accommodation to the line, tends to restrict their ability to engage in free, experimental innovation.

The CORRECT answer is:

5.____

A. 4, 2, 3, 1, 3　　　B. 1, 5, 3, 2, 4　　　C. 5, 3, 1, 2, 4
D. 2, 1, 4, 5, 3

———

KEY (CORRECT ANSWERS)

1. A
2. D
3. D
4. A
5. B

———

TEST 3

DIRECTIONS: Questions 1 through 4 consist of six sentences which can be arranged in a logical sequence. For each question, select the choice which places the numbered sentences in the *most logical* sequence. *PRINT THE LETTER OF THE CORRECT ANSWER IN THE SPACE AT THE RIGHT.*

1.
   1. The burden of proof as to each issue is determined before trial and remains upon the same party throughout the trial.
   2. The jury is at liberty to believe one witness' testimony as against a number of contradictory witnesses.
   3. In a civil case, the party bearing the burden of proof is required to prove his contention by a fair preponderance of the evidence.
   4. However, it must be noted that a fair preponderance of evidence does not necessarily mean a greater number of witnesses.
   5. The burden of proof is the burden which rests upon one of the parties to an action to persuade the trier of the facts, generally the jury, that a proposition he asserts is true.
   6. If the evidence is equally balanced, or if it leaves the jury in such doubt as to be unable to decide the controversy either way, judgment must be given against the party upon whom the burden of proof rests.

   The CORRECT answer is:

   A. 3, 2, 5, 4, 1, 6   B. 1, 2, 6, 5, 3, 4   C. 3, 4, 5, 1, 2, 6
   D. 5, 1, 3, 6, 4, 2

   1.____

2.
   1. If a parent is without assets and is unemployed, he cannot be convicted of the crime of non-support of a child.
   2. The term "sufficient ability" has been held to mean sufficient financial ability.
   3. It does not matter if his unemployment is by choice or unavoidable circumstances.
   4. If he fails to take any steps at all, he may be liable to prosecution for endangering the welfare of a child.
   5. Under the penal law, a parent is responsible for the support of his minor child only if the parent is "of sufficient ability."
   6. An indigent parent may meet his obligation by borrowing money or by seeking aid under the provisions of the Social Welfare Law.

   The CORRECT answer is:

   A. 6, 1, 5, 3, 2, 4   B. 1, 3, 5, 2, 4, 6   C. 5, 2, 1, 3, 6, 4
   D. 1, 6, 4, 5, 2, 3

   2.____

159

3. 1. Consider, for example, the case of a rabble rouser who urges a group of twenty people to go out and break the windows of a nearby factory.
    2. Therefore, the law fills the indicated gap with the crime of inciting to riot.
    3. A person is considered guilty of inciting to riot when he urges ten or more persons to engage in tumultuous and violent conduct of a kind likely to create public alarm.
    4. However, if he has not obtained the cooperation of at least four people, he cannot be charged with unlawful assembly.
    5. The charge of inciting to riot was added to the law to cover types of conduct which cannot be classified as either the crime of "riot" or the crime of "unlawful assembly."
    6. If he acquires the acquiescence of at least four of them, he is guilty of unlawful assembly even if the project does not materialize.

The CORRECT answer is:

A. 3, 5, 1, 6, 4, 2   B. 5, 1, 4, 6, 2, 3   C. 3, 4, 1, 5, 2, 6
D. 5, 1, 4, 6, 3, 2

3.____

4. 1. If, however, the rebuttal evidence presents an issue of credibility, it is for the jury to determine whether the presumption has, in fact, been destroyed.
    2. Once sufficient evidence to the contrary is introduced, the presumption disappears from the trial.
    3. The effect of a presumption is to place the burden upon the adversary to come forward with evidence to rebut the presumption.
    4. When a presumption is overcome and ceases to exist in the case, the fact or facts which gave rise to the presumption still remain.
    5. Whether a presumption has been overcome is ordinarily a question for the court.
    6. Such information may furnish a basis for a logical inference.

The CORRECT answer is:

A. 4, 6, 2, 5, 1, 3   B. 3, 2, 5, 1, 4, 6   C. 5, 3, 6, 4, 2, 1
D. 5, 4, 1, 2, 6, 3

4.____

KEY (CORRECT ANSWERS)

1. D
2. C
3. A
4. B

CPSIA information can be obtained
at www.ICGtesting.com
Printed in the USA
LVHW022059171219
640814LV00022B/436